Adobe® Illustrator® CC: Part 2

Adobe® Illustrator® CC: Part 2

Part Number: 092034
Course Edition: 9.0

Acknowledgements

PROJECT TEAM

Author	Media Designer	Content Editor
Gail Sandler	Brian Sullivan	Michelle Farney

Notices

DISCLAIMER

TRADEMARK NOTICES

Adobe® Illustrator® CC: Part 2

About This Course

You have created simple artwork by using the basic drawing and painting tools available in Adobe® Illustrator®. You now want to use advanced tools, options, and effects to create complex artwork. In addition, you want to ensure that your artwork is ready for commercial printing and also save it for the web. In this course, you will draw complex illustrations and enhance them by using various painting options. You will also use painting tools, manage colors, format type, work with effects, prepare artwork for commercial printing, and prepare graphics for the web.

This course is a great component of your preparation for the Adobe Certified Professional in Graphic Design & Illustration Using Adobe Illustrator exam.

Course Description

Target Student

This course is intended for designers, publishers, pre-press professionals, marketing communications professionals, or people taking on design responsibilities who need to use Illustrator to create illustrations, logos, advertisements, or other graphic documents. It is also useful for anyone interested in working toward the Adobe Certified Professional Graphic Design and Illustration Using Adobe Illustrator exam certification.

Course Prerequisites

To ensure your success in this course, you should be familiar with basic computer functions such as creating folders, launching programs, and working with Windows. You should also have basic Windows application skills, such as copying and pasting objects, formatting text, and saving files.

Familiarity with basic design terminology, such as palettes, color modes, shapes, text, and paths, is highly recommended.

You can obtain this level of skill and knowledge by taking the following Logical Operations course:

- *Adobe® Illustrator® CC: Part 1*

Course Objectives

Upon successful completion of this course, students will be able to use Adobe Illustrator to create complex illustrations, format illustrations and type, and prepare documents for print and web.

You will:

- Draw complex illustrations.
- Enhance artwork by using painting tools.

- Customize colors and swatches.
- Format type.
- Enhance the appearance of artwork.
- Prepare content for deployment.
- Set up project requirements.

The CHOICE Home Screen

Logon and access information for your CHOICE environment will be provided with your class experience. The CHOICE platform is your entry point to the CHOICE learning experience, of which this course manual is only one part.

On the CHOICE Home screen, you can access the CHOICE Course screens for your specific courses. Visit the CHOICE Course screen both during and after class to make use of the world of support and instructional resources that make up the CHOICE experience.

Each CHOICE Course screen will give you access to the following resources:

- **Classroom**: A link to your training provider's classroom environment.
- **eBook**: An interactive electronic version of the printed book for your course.
- **Files**: Any course files available to download.
- **Checklists**: Step-by-step procedures and general guidelines you can use as a reference during and after class.
- **LearnTOs**: Brief animated videos that enhance and extend the classroom learning experience.
- **Assessment**: A course assessment for your self-assessment of the course content.
- Social media resources that enable you to collaborate with others in the learning community using professional communications sites such as LinkedIn or microblogging tools such as Twitter.

Depending on the nature of your course and the components chosen by your learning provider, the CHOICE Course screen may also include access to elements such as:

- LogicalLABS, a virtual technical environment for your course.
- Various partner resources related to the courseware.
- Related certifications or credentials.
- A link to your training provider's website.
- Notices from the CHOICE administrator.
- Newsletters and other communications from your learning provider.
- Mentoring services.

Visit your CHOICE Home screen often to connect, communicate, and extend your learning experience!

How to Use This Book

As You Learn

This book is divided into lessons and topics, covering a subject or a set of related subjects. In most cases, lessons are arranged in order of increasing proficiency.

The results-oriented topics include relevant and supporting information you need to master the content. Each topic has various types of activities designed to enable you to solidify your understanding of the informational material presented in the course. Information is provided for reference and reflection to facilitate understanding and practice.

Data files for various activities as well as other supporting files for the course are available by download from the CHOICE Course screen. In addition to sample data for the course exercises, the course files may contain media components to enhance your learning and additional reference materials for use both during and after the course.

Checklists of procedures and guidelines can be used during class and as after-class references when you're back on the job and need to refresh your understanding.

At the back of the book, you will find a glossary of the definitions of the terms and concepts used throughout the course. You will also find an index to assist in locating information within the instructional components of the book.

As You Review

Any method of instruction is only as effective as the time and effort you, the student, are willing to invest in it. In addition, some of the information that you learn in class may not be important to you immediately, but it may become important later. For this reason, we encourage you to spend some time reviewing the content of the course after your time in the classroom.

As a Reference

The organization and layout of this book make it an easy-to-use resource for future reference. Taking advantage of the glossary, index, and table of contents, you can use this book as a first source of definitions, background information, and summaries.

Course Icons

Watch throughout the material for the following visual cues.

Icon	Description
	A **Note** provides additional information, guidance, or hints about a topic or task.
	A **Caution** note makes you aware of places where you need to be particularly careful with your actions, settings, or decisions so that you can be sure to get the desired results of an activity or task.
	LearnTO notes show you where an associated LearnTO is particularly relevant to the content. Access LearnTOs from your CHOICE Course screen.
	Checklists provide job aids you can use after class as a reference to perform skills back on the job. Access checklists from your CHOICE Course screen.
	Social notes remind you to check your CHOICE Course screen for opportunities to interact with the CHOICE community using social media.

1 | Drawing Complex Illustrations

Lesson Time: 1 hour

Lesson Introduction

You have experience creating relatively simple projects. Now, you can get started on design projects where you need to create complex illustrations. As the complexity of your projects increases, you will find it very difficult and time consuming to complete all your artwork with just the basic Adobe® Illustrator® features. Instead, you can apply several techniques that will let you create complex artwork from existing simple illustrations. In this lesson, you will draw complex illustrations.

Lesson Objectives

In this lesson, you will:

- Work with the grid and guides.

- Combine objects to create complex illustrations.

- Work with layers.

- Create a perspective drawing.

- Trace artwork.

TOPIC A

Apply the Grid, Guides, and Info Panel

Before beginning to draw complex illustrations, you may like to set up the artboard so that you can draw precise images. Illustrator provides several tools—such as the grid, guides, and rulers—that help you draw objects and align them accurately. In this topic, you will work with the grid and guides.

Grid and Guides

The *grid* is a collection of evenly spaced vertical and horizontal lines that appear at the background of artwork. It helps snap objects to the nearest pixel. *Guides* are additional horizontal and vertical lines that you can add to the document to help you align text and objects. You can create guides by dragging them from the horizontal and vertical rulers. By default, guides are hidden and they can be displayed when required. The grid and guides do not appear when the document is printed or displayed on the web.

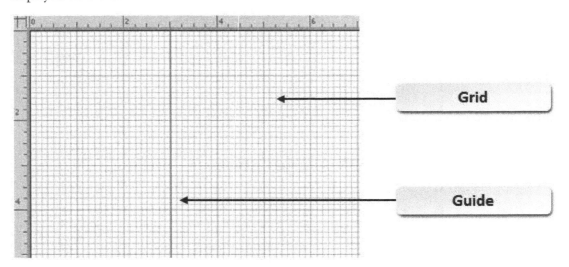

Figure 1–1: A document with a guide and the grid displayed.

Pixel Grid

The *pixel grid* is a set of vertical and horizontal lines that is used to align objects when you set pixels as the unit of measurement for your document. By using the pixel grid, you can ensure that objects begin and end on a whole pixel.

Smart Guides

Smart guides are temporary guides that help you align and transform objects relative to other objects. They appear when you draw, move, or transform an object. They are enabled by default and can be disabled if they are not required. Measurement labels that appear along with smart guides show information such as the X and Y coordinates of an object and the distance of an object from another object. The measurement labeled "dx" is the change in the object's horizontal position relative to the original position. The measurement labeled "dy" is the change in the object's vertical position relative to the original position. You can control the color and appearance of smart guides by setting their preferences.

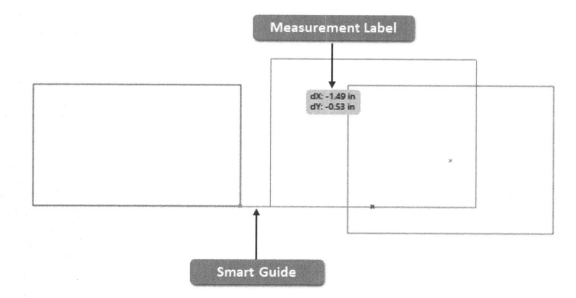

Figure 1–2: A smart guide that appears when one object is moved over another.

The Measure Tool

The **Measure** tool displays the distance between any two points. It can be found in the **Tools** panel, often hidden behind the **Eyedropper** tool. You can see the results in the **Info** panel. You can select the first point, and then drag to the second point. You can also Shift-drag to constrain the tool to multiples of 45 degrees. The **Info** panel then shows the following measurements:

* horizontal and vertical distances from the X and Y axes
* absolute horizontal and vertical distances
* total distances
* angle measured

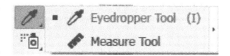

Figure 1–3: The Measure tool.

 Note: By default, the **Measure** tool is available in the **Essentials Classic** and **Typography** workspaces. You can manually add it to other workspaces if needed.

The Info Panel

The *Info panel* displays information about a selected object. It shows the X and Y coordinates and the dimensions of the object. When you use different tools, the **Info** panel displays additional information such as the change in X and Y coordinates, the distance the object is moved, percentage changes in the dimensions when the object is scaled, and the amount of shear. Exactly what information you get depends on the context and type of object selected. You can display the **Info** panel by selecting **Window→Info**.

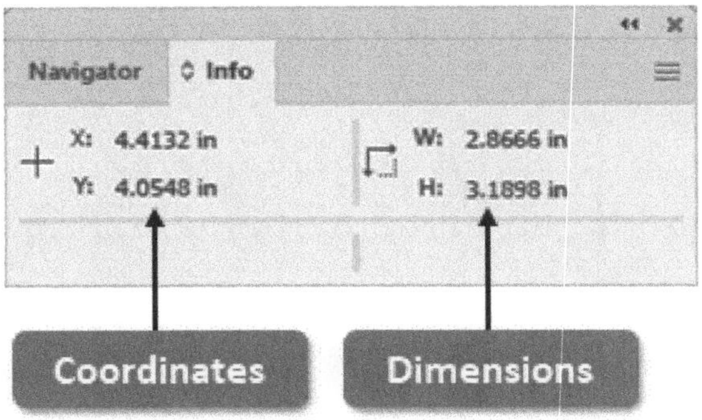

Figure 1-4: The Info panel.

 Note: The coordinates and dimensions are also available in the **Transform** section of the **Properties** panel and on the **Control** panel from the **Shape** section.

Access the Checklist tile on your CHOICE Course screen for reference information and job aids on How to Apply the Grid, Guides, and Info Panel.

ACTIVITY 1-1
Setting Guides and Grid Preferences

Scenario

The brochure you are about to create for Emerald Epicure will include several illustrations. You will use drawing tools to draw a lot of these illustrations on the artboard, and you need to make sure that all the illustrations are aligned accurately.

 Note: Activities may vary slightly if the software vendor has issued digital updates. Your instructor will notify you of any changes.

1. Start **Adobe Illustrator**.
   a) From the Windows taskbar, select the **Start** button.
   b) Select **Adobe Illustrator**.
      The **Home** screen is displayed when Illustrator is open and all documents are closed.

2. Create a new Illustrator document with the print settings you require for the brochure.
   a) Select the **New file** button.
   b) In the **New Document** dialog box, on the top bar, select **Print**.
   c) In the **PRESET DETAILS** pane, replace **Untitled-#** with *Emerald Epicure*
      The number after Untitled varies based on how many new documents you have created since starting Illustrator.
   d) In the **Number of Artboards** text box, change the number to *2*
   e) In the **BLANK DOCUMENT PRESETS** pane, select **A4**.

    Note: Notice that when you changed the preset, the number of artboards changed to the default value specified by the new **Blank Document Preset**.

   f) In the **Number of Artboards** text box, change the number to *2*
   g) From the **Units** drop-down list, select **Inches**.
   h) In the **Orientation** section, select **Landscape**.
   i) In the **Bleed** section, verify that the **Link** icon is selected so that all settings will be the same as the value you enter.
   j) In the **Top** text box, change the value to *0.5*
   k) Select **More Settings**.

l) In the **More Settings** dialog box, verify that the **Advanced** section contains the settings shown in this screenshot.

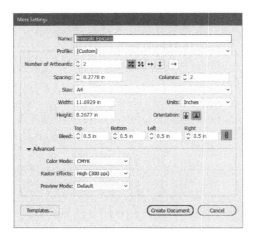

m) Select **Create Document**.

3. Specify preferences for guides and the grid.

a) Select **Edit→Preferences→Guides & Grid**.

b) In the **Guides** section, in the **Color** drop-down list, verify that **Cyan** is selected and in the **Style** drop-down list, verify that **Lines** is selected.

c) In the **Grid** section, in the **Subdivisions** text box, set the number to *10*

d) Verify that the **Grids In Back** check box is checked.

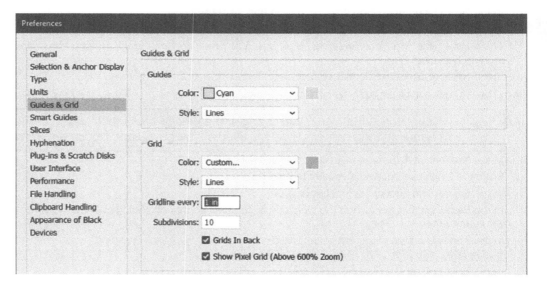

4. Specify preferences for smart guides.

a) In the left pane of the **Preferences** dialog box, select **Smart Guides**.

b) In the right pane, check the **Transform Tools** check box to display smart guides while transforming objects.

c) In the **Snapping Tolerance** text box, change the value to *3 pt* and select **OK**.

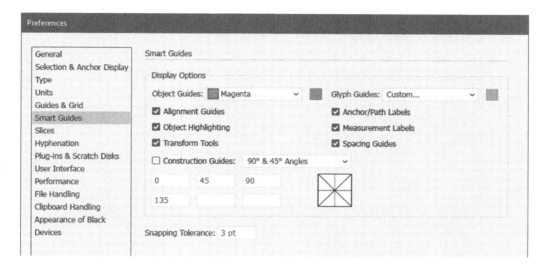

5. Display grid lines, guides, and rulers in your document.

   a) Select **View→Show Grid** to display grid lines.
   b) Select **View→Rulers→Show Rulers** to display the horizontal and vertical rulers.

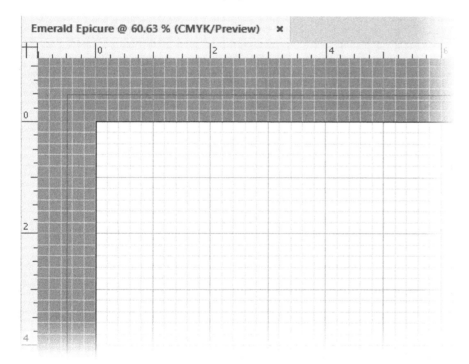

   c) From the vertical ruler, drag a guide to the **left** artboard and place it at a position exactly on the **6** inch mark on the horizontal ruler.
   d) Select the artboard on the right.
   e) On the status bar, from the **Zoom** menu, select **Fit On Screen**.
   f) From the vertical ruler, drag a guide to the **right** artboard and place it at a position exactly on the **6** inch mark on the horizontal ruler.

g) In the status bar, from the **Zoom** drop-down list, select **33.33%**.

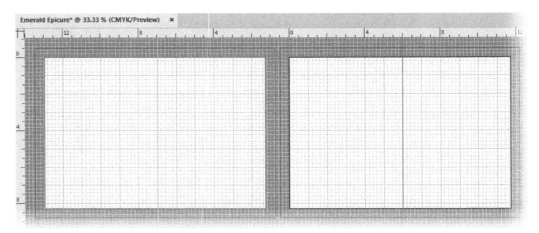

Both guides should be displayed.

6. Save the document.

a) Select **File→Save As**, then select **On your computer**.

b) In the **Save As** dialog box, navigate to the **C:\092034Data\Drawing Complex Illustrations** folder.

c) In the **File name** text box, type *My Grid Guide* and select **Save**.

d) In the **Illustrator Options** dialog box, select **OK** to accept the default settings.

e) Close the file.

TOPIC B

Combine Objects to Create Complex Illustrations

You customized your interface and can now access the tools you require to create complex illustrations. You can create complex illustrations quickly even if you are not an expert at drawing. One way of creating complex illustrations is by combining basic shapes such as rectangles and circles. Illustrator provides several tools that help you create illustrations by using existing objects. In this topic, you will combine objects to create complex illustrations.

Ways to Combine Objects

You can create complex illustrations by combining objects. Illustrator provides three ways to combine objects.

A complex illustration created by using compound shapes and pathfinder effects

A compound path

Figure 1–5: Examples of drawings created by combining simple shapes.

Way to Combine Objects	Description
Pathfinder Effects	Combines overlapping objects by using interaction modes. Illustrator provides ten interaction modes—four shape modes and six Pathfinder effects—in the **Pathfinder** panel. Interaction among the objects cannot be edited because the original objects are changed when the combined object is created.
Compound Shapes	Combines two or more objects by specifying how each object interacts with the other. Each object can be selected and edited. Interaction among objects can also be changed because the original objects are not changed.
Compound Paths	Combines objects by using one object to create a hole where it overlaps another. The paths that make up the combined object are treated as a single path. You can select and edit the individual objects of a compound path. You can also edit the combined path.

Shape Modes

Shape modes determine the areas of the selected objects that are to be combined. You can select shape modes from the **Pathfinder** panel. There are four shape modes.

Shape Mode	Description
Unite	Adds a shape to another shape that it overlaps.
Minus Front	Cuts the non-overlapping areas of the object in the front and combines the rest of the object with another object.
Intersect	Creates a shape out of the region where objects overlap.
Exclude	Traces an outline out of all the non-overlapping areas and creates a shape.

Pathfinder Effects

Pathfinder effects create new objects from overlapping objects. You can select Pathfinder effects from the **Pathfinder** panel. There are six Pathfinder effects.

Pathfinder Effect	Description
Divide	Separates artwork into filled components that can be edited independently.
Trim	Removes hidden regions of a filled object, removes strokes, and merges objects of different colors.
Merge	Removes hidden regions of a filled object. It also removes strokes and merges adjoining or overlapping objects of the same color.
Crop	Divides artwork into components and removes components that are outside the boundary of the object in the front.
Outline	Converts an object into path segments that can be edited independently.
Minus Back	Deletes objects at the back from the object in front.

Groups of Objects

Several objects can be combined into a group so that they are treated as a single unit. You can move or transform groups without affecting their attributes or relative positions. As an example, you might group objects together into a single logo design so that you can move and scale the entire logo. Grouped objects exist on the same layer, and are stacked in succession. You can choose to group or ungroup objects as desired.

Figure 1–6: Groups of objects.

The Shape Builder Tool

The *Shape Builder tool* allows you to create custom shapes out of two or more shapes. By using this tool, you can create shapes by selecting paths that you want to merge or by excluding paths that you do not require. By default, the **Shape Builder** tool is in the merge mode, enabling you to combine paths. You can remove regions within the selected shapes by entering into the erase mode.

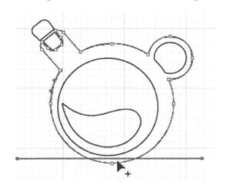

Original image with an overlapping line

Final image after applying the Shape Builder tool

Figure 1–7: A complex illustration edited by using a line and the Shape Builder tool.

The Pencil Tool

The *Pencil tool* helps you draw paths. It creates anchor points when you draw. Once you complete drawing, you can adjust the path by editing the anchor points. To access, click and hold the **Shaper** tool and select the **Pencil** tool. In addition to drawing paths, you can use the **Pencil** tool to add to a path, connect two paths, and reshape paths. The **Pencil** tool supports six options that help you specify settings for drawing and editing paths. You can access these options from the **Pencil Tool Options** dialog box by double-clicking the **Pencil** tool icon.

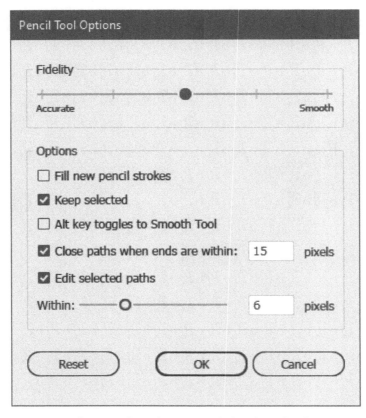

Figure 1-8: The Pencil Tool Options dialog box displaying options to customize the Pencil tool.

Pencil Tool Option	Description
Fidelity	Controls the spacing of anchor points as you draw a path. You can drag the slider from **Accurate** to **Smooth**.
Fill new pencil strokes	Applies a fill to newly drawn pencil strokes.
Keep selected	Determines whether the path is selected after you finish drawing it.
Alt key toggles to Smooth Tool	Use of the **Alt** key will change the action to that of the **Smooth** tool, which smooths shapes
Close paths when ends are within __ pixels	Paths close when ends are within a certain number of pixels.
Edit selected paths	Determines whether you can edit the selected path when the mouse pointer is close to the path.
Within	Sets the distance the pointer can be from the selected path to be able to edit it. This option is available only if the **Edit selected paths** option is selected.

Direction Lines and Points

Direction lines control the shape and size of curved segments in a path. They appear at anchor points and are always at a tangent to a curve. The angle of a direction line determines the slope of a curve and the length of a direction line determines the height and depth of a curve. Direction points are points at which direction lines end and are used to drag the direction lines. You can use direction lines and points to reshape the curved segments in a path.

The Navigator Panel

The *Navigator panel* displays a thumbnail view of your artwork and enables you to change the view of your document in the work area. It highlights the currently visible area of your document in a colored box called the proxy preview area. It also provides options to zoom in or out of any portion of the document.

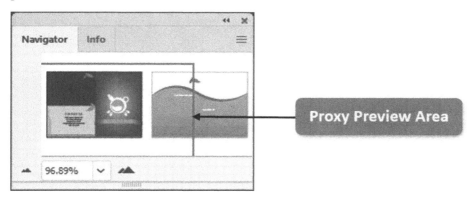

Figure 1-9: The Navigator panel displaying a portion of a document with two artboards.

You can customize the display area in the **Navigator** panel by setting the **Navigator** panel options.

Option	Purpose
Color	Sets color for the proxy preview area's border.
Greeking	Specifies the size of text in a document that can be displayed as legible characters in the **Navigator** panel. Text that is below this size is not legible.
Draw dashed lines as solid lines	Displays the dashed lines in the document as solid lines in the **Navigator** panel's preview.

View Artwork in Multiple Windows and Views

You can open a single document in multiple windows with each window displaying different views. By using the **Arrange** command in the **Window** menu, you can arrange multiple windows.

Intertwine

The **Intertwine** command provides a method to specify which parts of overlapping objects are in front of each other. This allows your design to have the illusion of depth within the artwork. If you only have two objects that you want to intertwine, select the objects, then select the highlighted boundary to make the intertwine with. If you have multiple overlapping objects with intersecting paths, you will need to specify where object boundaries are layered.

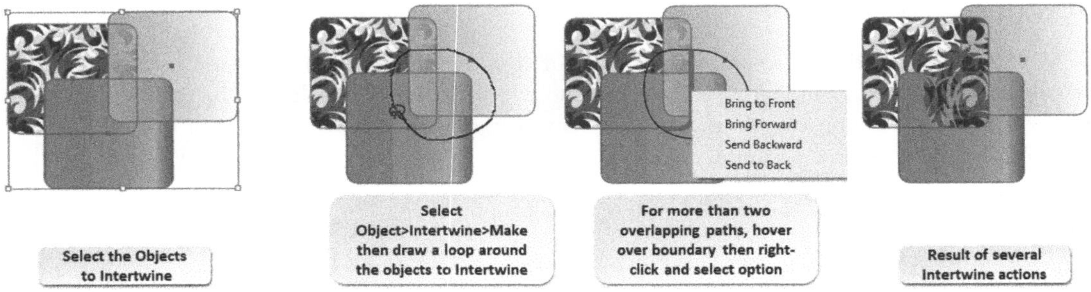

Select the Objects to Intertwine

Select Object>Intertwine>Make then draw a loop around the objects to Intertwine

For more than two overlapping paths, hover over boundary then right-click and select option

Bring to Front
Bring Forward
Send Backward
Send to Back

Result of several Intertwine actions

Figure 1-10: An example of intertwining objects with multiple overlapping boundary lines.

> **Access the Checklist tile on your CHOICE Course screen for reference information and job aids on How to Combine Objects to Create Complex Illustrations.**

ACTIVITY 1-2
Combining Objects to Create Complex Illustrations

Data File

C:\092034Data\Drawing Complex Illustrations\Emerald Epicure.ai

Scenario

You need to start creating illustrations for your brochure. On the outer page of your brochure, you want to have a picture of an olive oil bottle.

---

1. From the **Home** screen, open **C:\092034Data\Drawing Complex Illustrations \Emerald Epicure.ai**.

2. Set the workspace to **Essentials Classic**.

3. Verify that **Artboard Navigation** displays **1**. Select **Fit On Screen**.

4. Draw a circle to represent a bottle.
   a) On the **Tools** panel, select and hold the **Rectangle** tool, and from the menu, select the **Ellipse** tool.

      If a different shape tool was selected previously, select and hold on the current shape tool, then select the **Ellipse** tool.

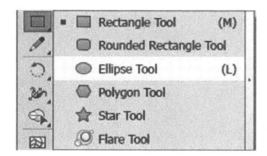

   b) Select on artboard **1** to display the **Ellipse** dialog box.
   c) In the **Ellipse** dialog box, in the **Width** text box, type *2*

d) In the **Height** text box, type *2* and select **OK** to create a circle with a diameter of **2** inches.

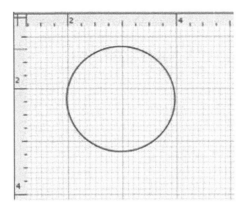

e) In the **Control Panel**, select **Transform**.

The **Transform** panel appears below the **Control Panel**. If you select anywhere else, the **Transform** panel closes. You can also access these settings in a separate **Transform** panel or in the **Properties** panel in the **Transform** section.

f) In the **Transform** panel, set X to *8.65* and Y to *4*

5. Draw an oil drop inside the circle to represent the contents of the bottle.

a) Make sure in the **Tools** panel that **Fill** is set to empty and **Stroke** is set to black.

b) In the **Tools** panel, from the **Shaper** tool flyout menu, select the **Pencil** tool .

c) Double-click the **Pencil** tool to open the **Pencil Tool Options** dialog box.

d) In the **Pencil Tool Options** dialog box, in the **Fidelity** section, move the slider to **Accurate** and select OK.

e) On the artboard, draw a drop of oil in the circle, similar to the following image.

You may wish to zoom in. You may have to try several times to get the shape the way you want it. If you do zoom in, be sure to zoom back out before proceeding.

6. Create the body of the bottle by combining two circles.
   a) In the **Tools** panel, select the **Ellipse** tool.
   b) Select the artboard to display the **Ellipse** dialog box.
   c) In the **Ellipse** dialog box, in the **Width** and **Height** text boxes, enter *1.625* and select OK.

d) Select the **Selection** tool and drag the circle, placing it within the first circle as follows.

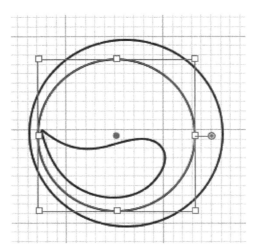

e) Select **Window→Pathfinder** to display the **Pathfinder** panel.
f) Select both circles. You should see two blue squares near the center of the circles.

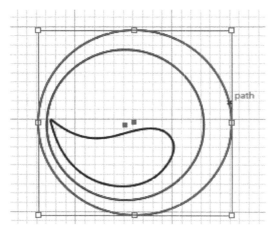

g) In the **Pathfinder** panel, in the **Shape Modes** section, select the **Minus Front** button (the second button) to combine the two circles into one object and remove the interior of the inner circle.

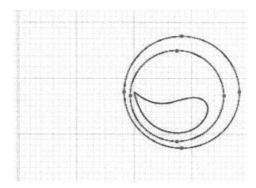

7. Draw the oil bottle's handle.

a) Draw a circle of diameter **0.72** inches.

b) Select the **Selection** tool and move the circle so that it overlaps the outer circle in its upper-right quadrant.

c) Draw a second smaller circle with a **0.55** inch diameter that fits inside the first one. Hold **Shift** and select the previously drawn circle to select both circles as shown.

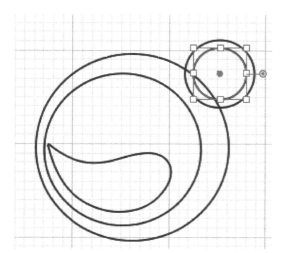

d) Make sure the **Pathfinder** pane is showing.

e) In the **Pathfinder** panel, select the **Minus Front** button 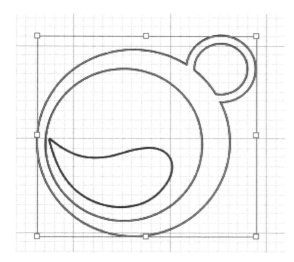 to combine the two circles.

f) Hold **Shift** and select the compound shape you created for the body of the bottle.

g) In the **Pathfinder** panel, select the **Unite** button.

8. Create a compound shape for the oil bottle's spout and cap.

a) Change the shape tool from the **Ellipse** tool to the **Rounded Rectangle** tool.

b) Draw a rounded rectangle similar to the one in the following image and position it on the bottle as shown. The size should be approximately **.4** inches wide, **.7** inches high, with a corner radius of about **.125** inches.

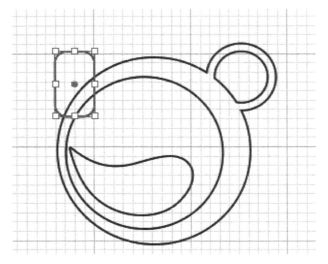

c) Create a smaller rounded rectangle about **.25** inches wide and **.4** inches high for the stopper and position it as shown.

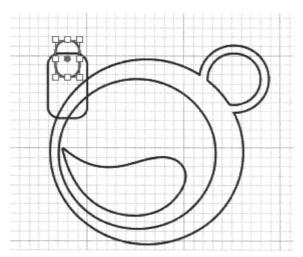

d) Zoom in on the image to about 600%.

e) Use the **Direct Selection** tool to select the anchor point at the lower-right side of the smaller rounded rectangle. Press the **Left Arrow** key twice to pull the lower-right side of the rectangle inward.

f) Similarly, select the anchor point at the lower-left side of the smaller rounded rectangle and press the **Right Arrow** key twice to pull the lower-left side of the rectangle inward.

g) Zoom out to **Fit On Screen** then verify your image is similar to that shown.

h) In the **Tools** panel, select the **Selection** tool.

i) Hold **Shift**, select both rectangles and, in the **Pathfinder** panel, select the **Divide** button to divide the smaller rectangle at the point where it intersects the larger rectangle.

9. Convert the rounded rectangles into the bottle's cap and spout.

a) Right-click the combined rounded rectangles, select **Ungroup**, and then click the artboard anywhere outside the graphic.

b) Use the **Selection** tool to select the top portion of the smaller rounded rectangle and drag it to the left to create a cap for the bottle.

c) In the **Transform** panel group, select the **Transform** panel.

d) Select the bottom portion of the small rounded rectangle that you divided, and in the **Transform** panel, in the **Width** text box, type *0.25* and in the **Height** text box, type *0.23*

e) Hold **Shift** and select the three objects that you created out of rounded rectangles.

    f)   Right-click the selected objects and select **Group**.

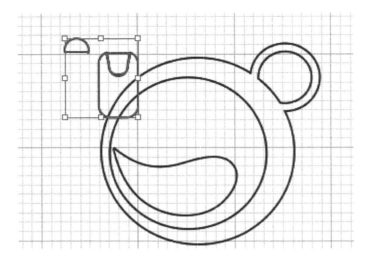

    g)   In the **Transform** panel, in the **Rotate** text box, type *40* and press **Enter**.

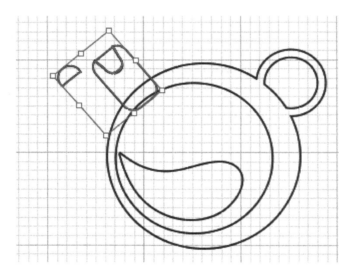

10. **Attach the spout to the bottle and position the cap above the spout.**

    a)   Right-click the grouped object and select **Ungroup**.

    b)   Click an empty area on the artboard to deselect the objects.

c) Use the **Selection** tool to move the cap of the bottle to a position above the object that is overlapping the bottle.

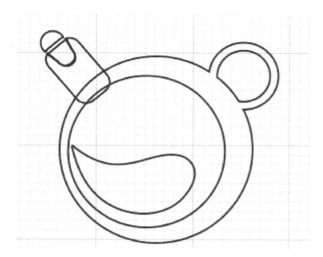

d) Select the spout, hold **Shift** and select the bottle.
e) In the **Pathfinder** panel, select the **Unite** button.

Your image should be similar to the following image.

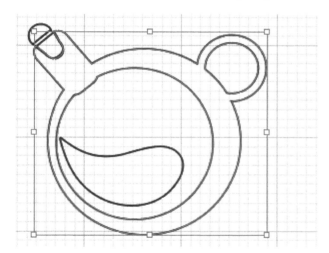

11. Create a flat base for the bottle.

a) In the **Tools** panel, select the **Line Segment** tool.
b) Select on the artboard to display the **Line Segment Tool Options** dialog box.
c) In the **Line Segment Tool Options** dialog box, in the **Length** text box, type *3* and in the **Angle** text box, type *0* and then select **OK**.

d) Use the **Selection** tool to move the line drawn on the artboard. Position the line so that it intersects the outer ring of the bottle but not the inner ring.

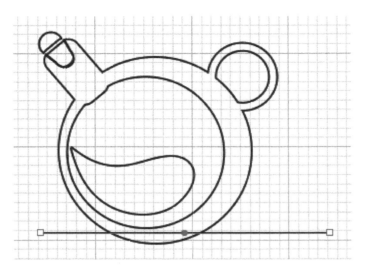

e) Hold **Shift** and select the bottle.

f) In the **Tools** panel, select the **Shape Builder** tool, hold **Alt**, and select the outer ring of the bottle that is below the line to delete that portion of the outer ring.

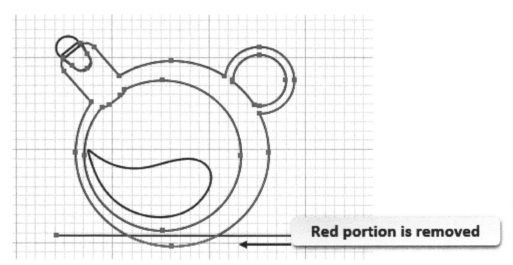

Red portion is removed

g) In the **Pathfinder** panel, select the **Unite** button to unite the overlapping portions of the bottle and line.

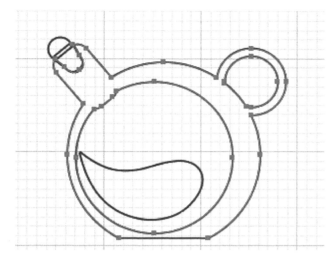

h) Save the file as *My Emerald Epicure.ai*
i) Leave the file open for the next activity.

TOPIC C

Organize Artwork with Layers

You created complex illustrations by combining objects. When you have several objects in a document, you will find it difficult to edit individual objects without affecting other objects. Placing objects in layers will enable you to edit them without affecting the rest of the document. In this topic, you will work with layers.

Layers

Layers are placeholders that contain one or more objects. They allow you to organize objects and edit them without affecting the other objects in a document. Layers help you arrange objects by changing their stacking order. You can use layers to lock, hide, and stack objects. The **Layers** panel displays the layers available in a document and provides options for managing layers.

If you have hidden layers and decide you no longer want those layers you can delete the hidden layers. In the **Layers** panel menu, you can select the option to delete the hidden layers and sublayers.

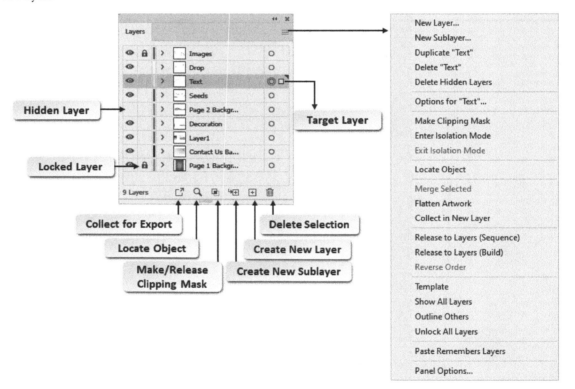

Figure 1-11: The Layers panel displaying layers in a document.

Object Hierarchy

When designating Illustrator document elements such as graphics and type, the decisions about where the elements lie is vital in creating an organized file. Establishing an intuitive and logical hierarchy can also save time. Before placing an item, think about where it should go and, if necessary, create a new layer for it. For instance, you know that you want your background to be in the back, so this will be the layer on the bottom. You generally want your text to be in the forefront, so your text will likely be the topmost layer.

Isolation Mode

The *Isolation mode* isolates a layer, a sublayer, a path, or groups of objects so that you can edit them without affecting other objects. It locks all the other objects in the document and disables them when you are editing. Once you exit the Isolation mode, Illustrator updates the object that you edited, making the changes permanent.

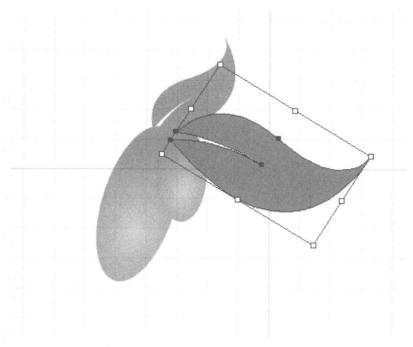

Figure 1–12: Isolation mode.

 Access the Checklist tile on your CHOICE Course screen for reference information and job aids on How to Organize Artwork with Layers.

ACTIVITY 1–3
Organizing Artwork with Layers

Before You Begin
My Emerald Epicure.ai is open.

Scenario
The portion below the oil bottle in the front page of your brochure is empty. You want to add some decorative objects in this space. However, you want to do this in such a way that the earlier artwork you created is not affected by the new objects you are about to create.

1. Create a layer.

    a) Select **Window→Layers** to display the **Layers** panel.

    b) In the **Layers** panel, select the **Create New Layer** button.

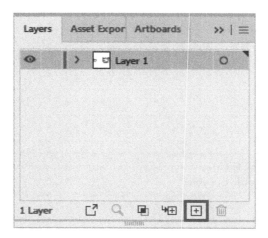

    c) Verify that a new layer named *Layer 2* is added.

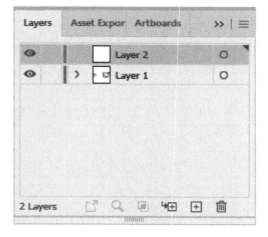

d) Double-click **Layer 2** and in the **Name** box, type *Decoration* and then press **Enter**.

2. Create an object in the **Decoration** layer.

   a) In the **Tools** panel, from the shapes tool menu, select the **Ellipse** tool.
   b) Click the artboard to display the **Ellipse** dialog box.
   c) In the **Ellipse** dialog box, in the **Width** text box, type *0.27*, in the **Height** box, type *.65*, and select OK.
   d) In the **Tools** panel, display the **Line Segment Tool** menu and select the **Spiral** tool. Then, click the artboard to display the **Spiral** dialog box.

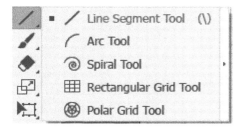

   e) In the **Spiral** dialog box, in the **Radius** text box, type *0.07* and in the **Segments** text box, type *5*

f)   In the **Style** section, verify that the left style option is selected and select **OK**.

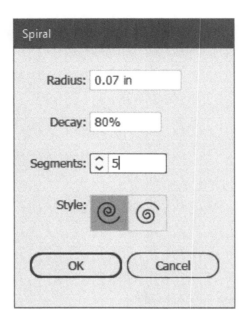

g)   Select the **Selection** tool, move the spiral within the ellipse, and position it on the top half of the ellipse.

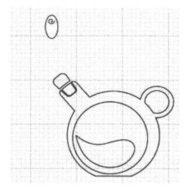

h)   In the **Transform** panel, in the **Rotate** text box, enter *-30* to rotate the spiral.
i)   Hold **Shift** and select the ellipse.
j)   Right-click the selection and select **Group**.

3. **Complete drawing objects below the bottle.**

a) Drag the group to the lower-right corner of the bottle.

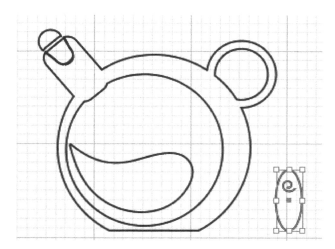

b) Copy the grouped object and paste it.
c) Move the copy adjacent to the original.
d) Rotate the objects so they appear similar to what is shown in the following graphic.

e) Group the two objects.
f) Copy and paste the group to create another set of ellipses with spirals, placing them as shown in the following graphic.

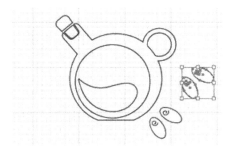

g) Select **Object→Transform→Reflect**.

h) In the **Reflect** dialog box, select OK.

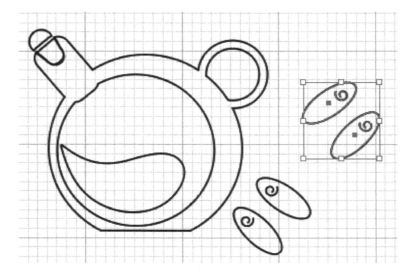

i) Move the reflected group to the lower-left of the bottle.

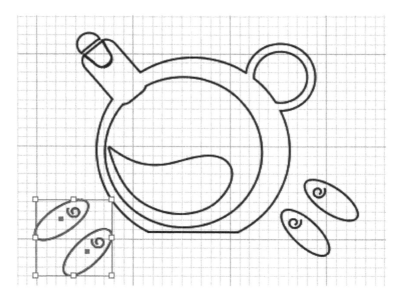

j) Save the changes to the file and leave it open for the next activity.

TOPIC D

Create a Perspective Drawing

You created drawings that are two-dimensional. If you want to create eye-catching images that resemble objects in the real world, you need to add depth to those images. You can do this in Illustrator by creating perspective drawings. In this topic, you will create a perspective drawing.

Perspective Theory

In graphics, perspective is an attempt to represent what the eye naturally sees on a flat, two-dimensional surface. Perspective gives a sense of depth and distance. The two most common features of perspective are:

- Objects get smaller as their distance from the observer increases.
- Along the line of sight, the size of the object's dimensions are relatively shorter than dimensions across the line of sight.

Perspective drawings have a horizon line (often implied) in which an object that moves farther and farther from the viewer, gets smaller and smaller until it vanishes. The scene will have a vanishing point that is usually directly opposite to the viewer's eye, and usually on the horizon.

Perspective Drawing

A *perspective drawing* is a two-dimensional image that has a sense of depth added to it. The objects in a perspective drawing appear to be nearer or farther depending on the angle and distance from which you view the drawing. If you view an object from a short distance, the object appears bigger than how it appears if you view it from a long distance.

There are three types of perspective drawings—one-point, two-point, and three-point. You can select the type of perspective drawing you want to draw in Illustrator. The default type of drawing is the two-point perspective.

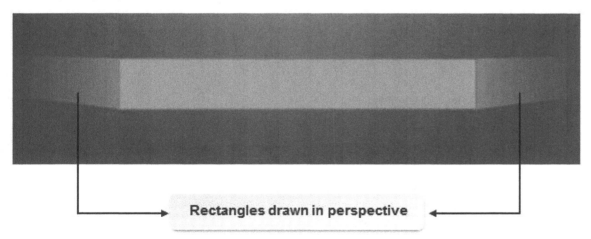

Figure 1–13: Rectangles drawn in perspective to add depth to an image.

 Note: To learn more about creating perspective drawings, check out the LearnTO **Create Perspective Drawings** presentation from the **LearnTO** tile on the CHOICE Course screen.

The Perspective Grid

The *perspective grid* is a set of grid lines that enable you to draw precise images in perspective. The point at which the lines in the perspective grid meet is called the vanishing point and the number of vanishing points in the grid depends on the type of perspective drawing you have selected. You can access the perspective grid by using the **Perspective Grid** tool. In a perspective grid, you can use grid lines, the **Perspective Selection** tool, and the **Active plane** widget to draw images in perspective.

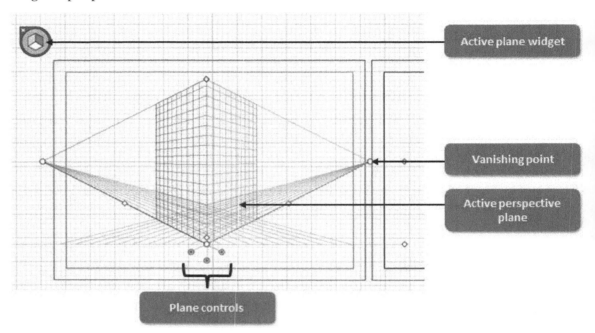

Figure 1-14: The perspective grid displayed on an Illustrator artboard.

Perspective Grid Presets

There are three perspective grid presets that define the perspective grid and provide the necessary settings to create one-point, two-point, and three-point perspective drawings. The three presets are **1P-Normal View**, **2P-Normal View**, and **3P-Normal View**. Each preset has several options that control the perspective grid. You can also create custom presets and save them.

Objects in Perspective

Once a perspective grid is created, you can also add elements to it so that those objects are also in perspective. To do so, you first select the desired object by using the **Perspective Selection** tool. You use a **Plane Switching Widget** to select the active grid plane. This allows you to create the observer's view of the scene.

You can move objects into perspective by using the **Perspective Selection** tool. To move objects more precisely, double-click the desired plane widget to open the left or right vanishing plane box. Automatic plane positioning allows you to automatically adjust the plane to match the height of the desired object. The **Perspective Selection** tool allows you to:

*   Bring text, objects, and symbols into perspective.
*   Switch active planes by using your keyboard.
*   Move, scale, or duplicate objects that are in perspective.

Text and Symbols in Perspective

You can also add text and symbols onto the perspective grid after it is created. To do so, you must first create the object you wish to add normally, not while in perspective mode. Once the text or symbol is created, use the **Perspective Selection** tool to drag it to the desired position on the active plane. You can edit text from the **Control** panel or by selecting **Object→Perspective**.

Although you can edit a simple definition on the perspective grid like you would in a flat plane, the symbol definition must have art that is supported in perspective. This would not include raster images, envelopes, and gradient meshes.

 Access the Checklist tile on your CHOICE Course screen for reference information and job aids on How to Create a Perspective Drawing.

ACTIVITY 1-4
Creating a Perspective Drawing

Before You Begin
My Emerald Epicure.ai is open.

Scenario
You want to enhance the look of the front cover of your brochure by adding objects that appear to have depth. You want to do this by creating a rectangular band in perspective on which colors fade out gradually.

1. **Create rectangles required for the brochure cover.**
   a) In the **Tools** panel, from the shapes tool menu, select the **Rectangle** tool.
   b) Click the artboard to display the **Rectangle** dialog box.
   c) In the **Rectangle** dialog box, in the **Width** text box, enter *3.65* and in the **Height** text box, enter *0.54* and then select **OK**.
   d) Drag the rectangle and position it below the bottle at the vertical center of the front cover of your brochure.

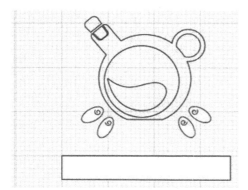

   e) Create two rectangles with a width of **1.25** inches and a height of **0.38** inches, and position them above the bottle one below the other.

2. **Set up the perspective grid.**
   a) Switch to the **Typography** workspace.

      The Basic **Typography** workspace doesn't contain the **Perspective Grid** tool. You can either add it to the workspace, or switch to the Advanced version of the **Typography** workspace.

b) In the **Tools** panel, select the **Edit Toolbar** button.

c) In the **All Tools** drawer, from the flyout menu, select **Advanced**.

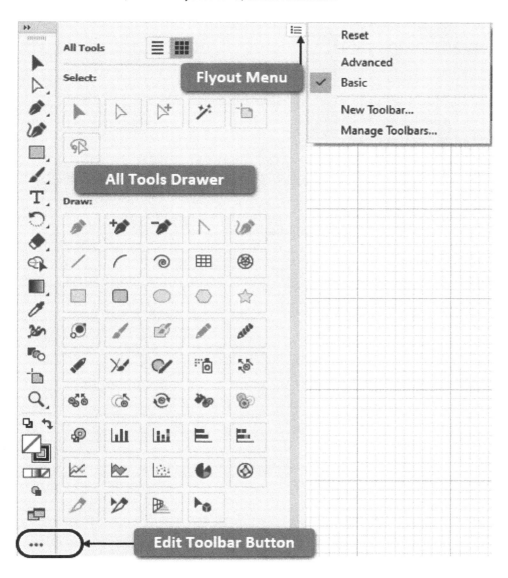

d) Select the **Perspective Grid** tool to display the perspective grid.

e) Scroll down to the right until you can view the resizing handles of the perspective grid.
f) If on the horizontal ruler the numbering restarts at the left edge of Artboard 2, right-click the horizontal ruler and select **Change to Global Rulers**.

g) Select the resizing handle at the bottom-right corner of the perspective grid and drag it to the intersection of approximately **11** inches on the vertical ruler and **16.8** inches on the horizontal ruler to position the grid. Observe that the plane controls are now below the bottom edge of Artboard 1.

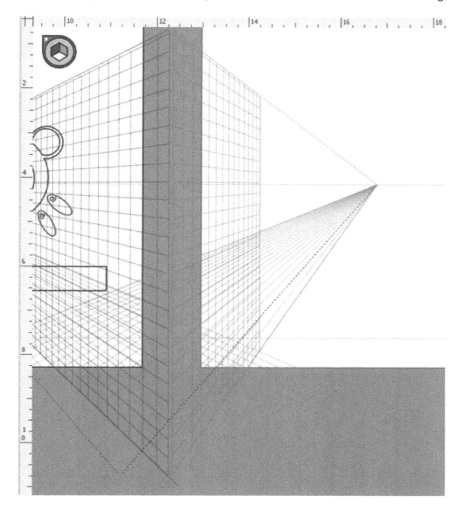

h) Scroll up to the left so that the guide appears immediately to the right of the **Tools** panel.

i) Use the **Selection** tool to select the topmost rectangle above the bottle.

j) In the **Tools** panel, display the **Perspective Grid Tool** menu and select the **Perspective Selection** tool.

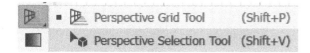

k) On the **Active Plane Widget**, select the right face of the cube. The selected face is orange and corresponds to the grid color.

3. Place two rectangles in perspective.

a) Drag the selected rectangle and position it on the perspective grid so that its left edge is aligned to the right edge of the big rectangle that is below the bottle.

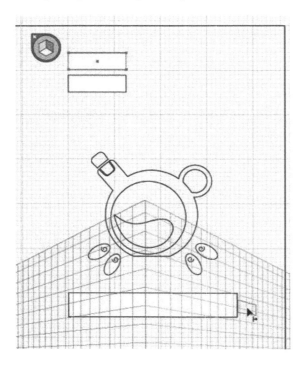

b) Use the resizing handles of the rectangle that is in perspective to transform it so that its left edge is of the same size as the right edge of the big rectangle and its right edge touches the edge of the artboard.

c) Use the **Selection** tool to select the other rectangle on the top of the artboard.
d) In the **Tools** panel, select the **Perspective Selection** tool.

e) On the **Active Plane Widget**, select the left face of the cube. The selected face is blue and corresponds to the grid color.
f) Drag the selected rectangle and position it to the left of the big rectangle that is below the bottle.

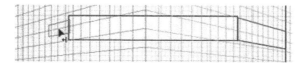

g) Use the resizing handles of the rectangle to transform it so that its right edge is of the same size as the left edge of the big rectangle and its left edge touches the 6" vertical gridline marking on the artboard.

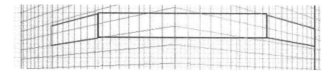

h) Select **View→Perspective Grid→Hide Grid**.
i) Save the changes to the file and leave it open for the next activity.

TOPIC E

Trace Artwork

You created perspective drawings to add realism to your artwork. Another method of adding realism is through use of artwork similar to photographs. To draw photo-like images from scratch will be next to impossible. But, you can trace such images by using the tracing features available in Illustrator. In this topic, you will trace artwork.

The Image Trace Command

The *Image Trace* command traces a raster graphic such as a bitmap and creates a vector illustration based on that graphic. Once the raster graphic is traced, you can convert the vector artwork to paths and edit it. Illustrator provides image trace presets for specific types of artwork. You can also create custom presets.

Original image   **Traced image**

Figure 1–15: A raster image and its traced vector image.

 Note: The **Live Trace** command in earlier versions of Illustrator has been replaced by the **Image Trace** command.

The Image Trace Panel

The **Image Trace** panel provides options for applying image trace presets and specifying tracing options that control the conversion of a raster image to a traced vector illustration.

Tracing Options

By using the tracing options in the **Image Trace** panel, you can control the way the **Image Trace** command traces artwork.

Tracing Option	Used To
Preset	Specify the tracing preset. You can also copy a default preset, create a custom preset, and rename or delete a custom preset.
View	Display the original image, the tracing result, or outlines.
Mode	Set the color mode for the traced resultant image.
Palette	Apply a palette of colors depending on the selected mode.
Color Settings	Specify the number of colors, number of grays, and threshold limits for a black and white tracing result.
Paths	Set the tightness of the path fitting to the original pixel shape.
Corners	Specify the amount of corners in the tracing result.
Noise	Specify a region in the original image that is to be ignored while tracing.
Method	Specify the tracing method. You can choose the abutting method to create cutout paths or the overlapping method to create stacked paths.
Fills	Apply fills to regions in the tracing result.
Strokes	Apply strokes to paths in the tracing result.
Snap Curve to Lines	Specify whether slightly curved lines are to be converted to straight lines.
Ignore White	Specify whether areas filled with white are to be made transparent.

Path, Corner, and Noise Reduction

In the **Image Trace** panel, in the **Advanced** section, you can access tools to refine the image trace. These options include path corner and noise reduction. The **Path** slider will make the path fit tighter or looser in relation to the original. The slider for **Corners** will make them more or less round. And finally the **Noise** option will increase or decrease the background **Noise** that might exist in the original image.

 Access the Checklist tile on your CHOICE Course screen for reference information and job aids on How to Trace Artwork.

ACTIVITY 1-5
Tracing a Photograph

Data File

C:\092034Data\Drawing Complex Illustrations\Jar.png

Before You Begin

The My Emerald Epicure.ai file is open.

The Typography workspace is selected.

Scenario

You are searching for an image of a jar that you want to show on the outer cover of your brochure. There is no vector illustration of a jar available in your company's graphics library. However, there is a photograph of a jar that you think would suit your brochure cover.

1. Place the image of the jar in your document.
   a) Scroll to the bottom-left corner of the artboard.
   b) Select **File→Place**.
   c) In the **Place** dialog box, navigate to the **C:\092034Data\Drawing Complex Illustrations** folder and place **Jar.png** on the artboard.
   d) Drag the image of the jar to the bottom-left corner of the artboard and place it so that the jar's left and bottom edges align with the left and bottom margins of the artboard, respectively.

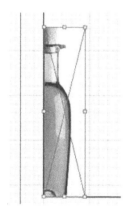

2. Trace the jar to a vector graphic.
   a) Select **Window→Image Trace** to display the **Image Trace** panel.
   b) In the **Image Trace** panel, from the **Preset** drop-down list, select **Silhouettes**.

c) If the image was not automatically traced, select **Trace**.

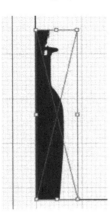

d) Close the **Image Trace** panel.
e) Save and close the file

Summary

In this lesson, you created complex illustrations. Creating complex artwork by combining simple objects, tracing raster graphics, or adding depth to your drawings not only saves you a lot of time and effort, but also lets you create realistic illustrations.

Give instances of complex illustrations that you may need to create and the techniques you would need to use to create them.

Suppose you need to create a logo. What options would you use to create the logo by combining simple shapes?

 Note: Check your CHOICE Course screen for opportunities to interact with your classmates, peers, and the larger CHOICE online community about the topics covered in this course or other topics you are interested in. From the Course screen you can also access available resources for a more continuous learning experience.

2 Enhancing Artwork Using Painting Tools

Lesson Time: 1 hour, 15 minutes

Lesson Introduction

You created complex illustrations by using different drawing techniques. Now, you may want to enhance those illustrations by painting them with beautiful fills and strokes. In this lesson, you will use painting tools to enhance artwork.

Lesson Objectives

In this lesson, you will:

- Paint objects with fills and strokes.

- Paint objects by using Live Paint groups.

- Paint with custom brushes.

- Apply transparency and blending modes.

- Apply meshes to objects.

- Apply patterns.

TOPIC A

Paint Objects Using Fills and Strokes

You created complex illustrations. As you work on more challenging design projects, you will need more control over the way your artwork is painted. Adobe® Illustrator® provides several tools and options that help you control the way your objects are painted and enhance their appearance. In this topic, you will paint objects with fills and strokes.

Fill and Stroke Controls

Fill and stroke controls enable you to control the fill and stroke applied to an object. You can access these controls from the **Tools** panel, the **Control** panel, and the **Color** panel.

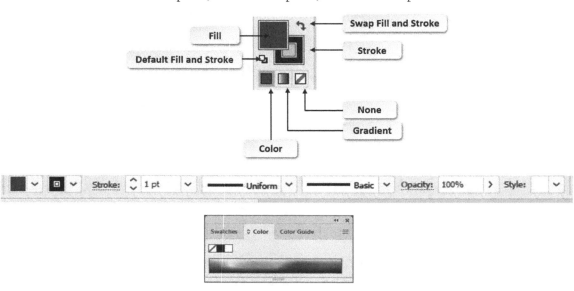

Figure 2–1: Fill and Stroke controls in the Tools panel.

Fill and Stroke Control	Description
Fill	Displays the Color Picker for selecting the fill color.
Stroke	Displays the Color Picker for selecting the stroke color.
Swap Fill and Stroke	Swaps the fill color and stroke color.
Default Fill and Stroke	Select to reset to default colors for fill and stroke. The default fill color is white and the default stroke color is black.
Color	Applies the last-selected color to an object.
Gradient	Changes the fill to the last-selected gradient.
None	Removes the selected object's fill or stroke.

The Blob Brush Tool

The *Blob Brush* tool 🖌 creates filled paths that can merge with other objects of the same fill color. While drawing paths, the **Blob Brush** tool merges new paths with the path having the same fill color in the top-most layer that it encounters. If the new path encounters more than one matching path, then the **Blob Brush** tool merges all the intersecting paths together. The **Blob Brush** tool cannot create paths with strokes.

Figure 2-2: An object created by using the Blob Brush tool.

By default, the **Blob Brush** tool uses the same brush options as calligraphic brushes. You can change these brush options to customize the **Blob Brush** tool.

Blob Brush Tool Option	Description
Keep Selected	Specifies that all the selected paths remain selected until you complete painting with the **Blob Brush** tool.
Merge Only with Selection	Specifies that new paths merge only with paths that are already selected.
Fidelity	Controls the distance at which new anchor points are added as you paint with the **Blob Brush**. Use the slider to change the setting from Accurate to Smooth.
Size	Specifies the size of the brush.
Angle	Sets the angle of rotation for the brush.
Roundness	Specifies the roundness of the brush.

Fill and Stroke Removal

Removing the **Fill** or **Stroke** from an object is as simple as adding a new one. First select the object, then in the **Tools** panel, select the **Fill** box or the **Stroke** box. Then in the **Tools** panel, **Color** panel, or the **Swatches** panel, select the **None** option.

Multiple Fills and Strokes

Multiple fills and strokes can be added to an Illustrator element from the **Appearance** panel. Doing so can increase the visual appeal of an object. It can also create more depth for a three-dimensional look. To do this select the object or objects and then from the **Appearance** panel menu, select **Add New Fill** or **Add New Stroke**. You will then set the color, stroke size, and/or opacity level.

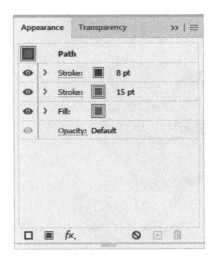

Figure 2–3: One circle with two different color strokes and one color fill.

Gradients

A *gradient* is a coloration technique that transitions from one color to another in a given direction. Some gradients are linear; that is, they go from point A to point B by gradually shifting the presence of one color with another in a very subtle, smooth way. Other gradients are radial; that is, they transition from one color inward to a central point of interest. You can also alter the angle and aspect ratio of a gradient.

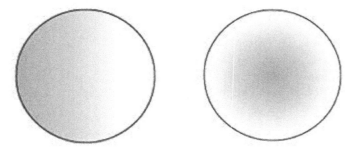

Figure 2–4: Linear and radial gradients.

Freeform Gradients

In addition to linear and radial gradients, Illustrator enables you to create *freeform gradients*, or graduated blends of color in an ordered or random sequence. There are two modes for freeform gradients: point mode and line mode. While you can apply linear and radial gradients to an object's fill and stroke, freeform gradients can be applied only to an object's fill.

Figure 2-5: A freeform gradient that uses a random blend of color.

Modified Gradients

Gradients do not have to have an utterly smooth transition between colors. Transitions can take place at different rates to achieve the desired effect.

Figure 2-6: A modified gradient.

 Access the Checklist tile on your CHOICE Course screen for reference information and job aids on How to Paint Objects Using Fills and Strokes.

ACTIVITY 2–1
Painting Objects with Gradients and Filled Paths

Data File

C:\092034Data\Enhancing Artwork Using Painting Tools\Emerald Epicure.ai

Scenario

The objects on the front cover of your brochure and the background are dull and unattractive. You want to fill the background and objects with beautiful colors and gradients. In addition, you want to create a drawing of a leaf attached to a stem for the back cover of your brochure.

---

1. Open **C:\092034Data\Enhancing Artwork Using Painting Tools\Emerald Epicure.ai.**

2. Set the workspace to **Essentials** in **Advanced** mode.
   a) On the **Application** menu, select the **Essentials** workspace.
   b) In the **Toolbar**, select **Edit Toolbar**.
   c) Select the panel menu in the upper-right corner of the menu, then select **Advanced**.

3. Create a background for the front cover of the brochure.
   a) In the **Layers** panel, select the **Create New Layer** button to create a new layer.
   b) Double-click **Layer 5** and enter *Page 1 Background*
   c) Select and drag the **Page 1 Background** layer to place it below **Layer 1**.

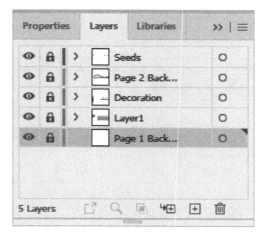

   d) Select the **lock** icon for **Page 1 Background** to unlock the layer and make it editable.

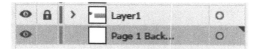

   e) Collapse the docks that contain the various panel groups so that you can view more of the artboard.
   f) Draw a rectangle with a width of **5.7** inches and a height of **8.25** inches.

g) Drag the rectangle over the oil bottle so that the right edge of the rectangle aligns with the right edge of the artboard.

h) In the **Tools** panel, double-click the **Fill** control.

i) In the **Color Picker** dialog box, in the **#** text box, type *006532* and select **OK**.

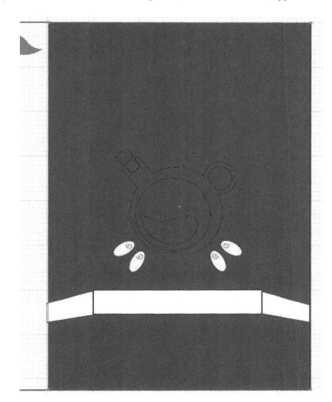

4. Apply a color to the rectangle below the oil bottle.

a) In the **Layers** panel, unlock the **Decoration** layer.

b) In the set of rectangles below the oil bottle, select the big rectangle.

c) In the **Swatches** panel, select the third color (green) in the second row.

5. Apply a gradient to one of the rectangles on the perspective drawing.

a) Select the rectangle that is drawn in perspective to the right of the big rectangle.

b) Select the **Gradient** panel.

c) In the **Gradient** panel, for **Type**, select **Linear Gradient**.

d) At the right end of the **Gradient** slider, double-click the gradient stop.

e) Select the **Swatches** button on the left side of the box that appears.

f) In the set of swatches displayed, select the third color (dark green) in the second row.

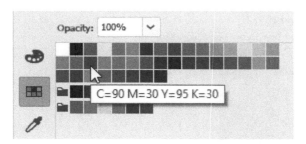

g) At the left edge of the **Gradient** slider, double-click the gradient stop, and in the set of swatches that appears, select the first color in the second row. It is not critical for it to be perfect—make the gradient look something like this.

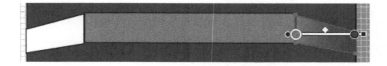

6. **Apply a gradient to the other rectangle on the perspective drawing.**
   a) Select the rectangle that is drawn in perspective to the left of the big rectangle.
   b) In the **Gradient** panel, for **Type**, select **Linear Gradient**.
   c) In the **Gradient** panel, select the **Reverse Gradient** button ![btn] to interchange the two gradient stops.

7. **Apply a gradient to the strokes of the rectangles.**
   a) Select the big rectangle at the center.
   b) In the **Tools** panel, select the **Stroke** button.
   c) In the **Gradient** panel, for **Type**, select **Linear Gradient**.
   d) In the **Stroke** section, verify that the **Apply gradient within stroke** button is selected.
   e) In the **Gradient** slider, for the left gradient stop, select the first color in the second row. For the right gradient stop, select the second color in the second row of swatches.
   f) Similarly, apply the same gradient to the strokes of the small rectangles on either side of the big rectangle.

   g) Deselect all objects.

8. **Create a leaf by using the Blob Brush tool (located in the Paintbrush tool flyout).**
   a) Set the stroke color as **None**.

b) In the **Tools** panel, select the **Fill** button, and in the **Swatches** panel, select the fifth color in the second row.

c) From the **Paintbrush Tool** flyout menu, select the **Blob Brush** tool.

d) In the **Tools** panel, double-click the **Blob Brush** tool.

e) In the **Blob Brush Tool Options** dialog box, drag the **Fidelity** slider to the right to **Smooth**.

f) In the **Size** text box, enter *1* and select **OK**.

g) Draw a leaf similar to the upper leaf shown in the following image.

9. Fill the leaf and merge it with the existing leaf.

a) Set the stroke color to **None**. Set the fill color to green.

b) Double-click the **Blob Brush** tool.

c) In the **Blob Brush Tool Options** dialog box, in the **Size** text box, enter *3* and select **OK**.

d) Paint the newly created leaf and the portions where the new leaf and existing leaf intersect to merge the two leaves.

> **Note:** Adjust the size of the brush stroke as required. You can also increase the Zoom percentage if you are comfortable with a magnified view of the artboard.

e) Use the **Pencil** tool, with white as the stroke color, to create a vein for the leaf.

f) Choose **File→Save As**.

g) Navigate to the **C:\092034Data\Enhancing Artwork Using Painting Tools** folder and save the file as *My Emerald Epicure.ai*

h) In the **Illustrator Options** dialog box, accept the default options and select **OK**.

i) Leave the file open for the next activity.

TOPIC B

Paint Objects Using Live Paint Groups

You used fills and strokes to paint objects and paths. However, you may want more flexibility and control over how the different areas in your illustrations are painted. By using Live Paint groups, you can paint complex objects with varying strokes and fills for different parts of the object while having complete control over how each area of the object is painted. In this topic, you will use Live Paint groups to paint objects.

Live Paint Groups

A *Live Paint group* is a set of editable paths that intersect to divide the drawing surface into areas that can be painted. The areas in a Live Paint group are called edges and faces. An edge is a path that divides two intersecting areas. A face is the area enclosed by one or more edges. You can apply different fills and strokes to individual faces and edges of a Live Paint group. When you adjust a path in a Live Paint group, the fills and strokes you applied on the faces and edges are reapplied to the modified faces and edges.

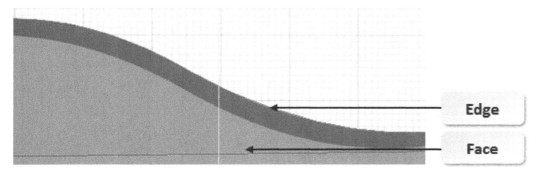

Figure 2-7: A Live Paint group consisting of a set of curved paths and straight lines.

The Live Paint Selection Tool

The **Live Paint Selection** tool is used to select individual faces and edges in a Live Paint group and fill them with the currently selected fill color. As you move the mouse pointer over a component in a Live Paint group, the **Live Paint Selection** tool's pointer changes to indicate whether the component is a face or an edge.

The Live Paint Bucket Tool

The *Live Paint Bucket* tool is used to paint the faces and edges of Live Paint groups with fills and strokes. It uses the currently selected fill and stroke attributes to paint faces and edges. You can use the **Live Paint Bucket** tool to reapply the fills and strokes to faces and edges in a Live Paint group.

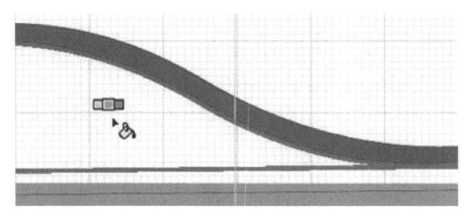

Figure 2-8: The Live Paint Bucket tool.

Live Paint Bucket Options

Live Paint Bucket options help you control the way the **Live Paint Bucket** tool paints faces and edges with fill and strokes.

Live Paint Bucket Options	Description
Paint Fills	Allows faces to be painted.
Paint Strokes	Allows edges to be painted.
Cursor Swatch Preview	Displays a preview of three colors when you move the mouse pointer over a face to be filled. The three colors are the selected color, the color to the left of the selected color in the **Swatches** panel, and the color to the right of the selected color in the **Swatches** panel.
Highlight	Highlights the faces and edges when you move the cursor over them. Faces and edges are highlighted with thick and thin lines, respectively.
Color	Specifies the color for the highlight.
Width	Sets the thickness of the highlight.

Live Paint Limitations

In a Live Paint group, fills and strokes are applied to faces and edges and not paths in the drawing. Therefore, you can apply features such as transparency, effects, multiple fills and strokes, object distortion, rasterization, slices, opacity masks, and brushes to the entire Live Paint group and not on individual faces and edges.

 Access the Checklist tile on your CHOICE Course screen for reference information and job aids on How to Paint Objects Using Live Paint Groups.

ACTIVITY 2-2
Painting Objects Using Live Paint Groups

Before You Begin

My Emerald Epicure.ai is open.

The Essentials workspace is selected and shown in Advanced mode.

Scenario

The third page of your brochure contains a green background at the bottom half, a set of curved paths, and a straight line at the top. These curved paths and the straight line are adjacent to each other. You want to apply different colors to each of the regions enclosed by these paths and the straight line so that they combine together to form a beautiful background for the top half of the page.

---

1. **Convert the set of curved paths and straight lines to a Live Paint group.**

   a) From the **Artboards** navigation list, select artboard **2** and then select **Fit On Screen** so that the artboard on the right is entirely visible.

   b) In the **Layers** panel, unlock **Page 2 Background**.

   c) In the **Tools** panel, select the **Selection** tool.

   d) Hold **Shift** and select the two curved paths and two straight lines above the green-colored rectangle. All four objects (shown in purple) should be selected.

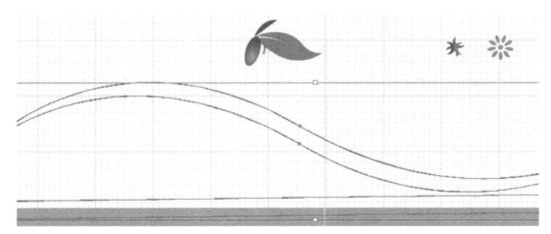

   e) Select **Object→Live Paint→Make**.

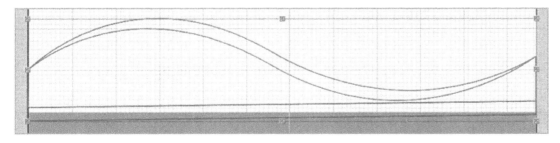

   The selection handles change to indicate the **Live Paint** group.

---

2. Fill the area between the curved paths in the Live Paint group with green.

   a) In the **Tools** panel, from the **Shape Builder** tool menu, select the **Live Paint Selection** tool.

   b) Move the mouse over the face between the curved paths and observe that a red outline appears around the face to highlight it.

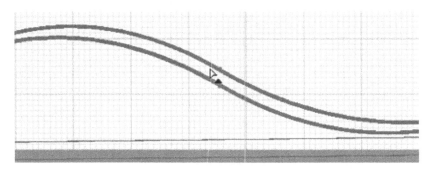

   c) Click the face to select it.

   d) In the **Swatches** panel, select the sixth color (dark green) in the second row.

   e) Observe that the selected face of the Live Paint group is painted with the selected color.

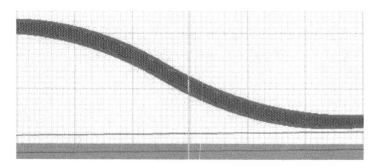

3. Fill the area below the curved paths in the Live Paint group using the **Live Paint Bucket** tool.

   a) In the **Tools** panel, from the **Live Paint Selection** tool menu, select the **Live Paint Bucket** tool.

   b) In the **Swatches** panel, select the fourth color (green) in the second row.

   c) Move the mouse over the face just below the curved path and notice that the area is surrounded by a thick red border.

   d) Click the face to fill it with the selected color.

4. Fill the face between the line and the green rectangle at the bottom by using the **Live Paint Bucket** tool.

   a) Move the mouse pointer below the horizontal line in the Live Paint group, and when the cursor changes to a bucket, click to fill the face with the selected color.

   b) In the **Tools** panel, select the **Selection** tool to deactivate the **Live Paint Bucket** tool.

   c) Select the **Live Paint** group.

   d) In the **Tools** panel, select the **Stroke** button.

e) Select **None** to remove strokes from the **Live Paint** group. Change to the **Selection** tool and verify your screen matches the following image.

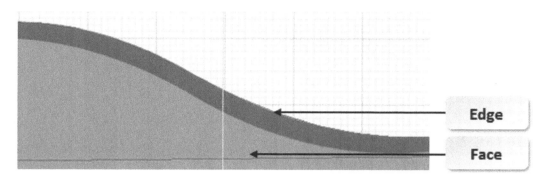

f) Save the file and leave it open for the next activity.

TOPIC C

Paint with Custom Brushes

You used Live Paint groups to paint paths with the freedom of using varying strokes and fills. You may want to enhance your artwork further by applying brush strokes that look natural. In this topic, you will paint with custom brushes.

Types of Brushes

There are five types of brushes that enable you to style the paths in artwork.

Brush Type	Description
Calligraphic	Creates brush strokes similar to strokes drawn by using a calligraphic pen.
Scatter	Paints a path by creating copies of an object such as a star or flower.
Art	Applies brush strokes on a path by stretching the brush shape or an object along the length of the path.
Bristle	Creates brush strokes that appear similar to strokes applied with a natural brush that uses bristles.
Pattern	Paints a path by using a pattern that repeats along the path.

Paintbrush Tool Options

You can set options for the **Paintbrush** tool to control the way it paints paths.

Paintbrush Tool Option	Description
Fidelity	Controls the spacing of anchor points as you draw a path with the paint brush. You can set a value between 0.5 and 20 pixels.
Smoothness	Specifies the amount of smoothing. You can set a percentage value between 0 and 100.
Fill New Brush Strokes	Applies a fill to newly drawn paths.
Keep Selected	Determines whether a path remains selected after you finish drawing it.
Edit Selected Paths	Determines whether you can edit a selected path.
Within	Sets the distance the mouse pointer can be from the selected path to be able to edit it. This option is available only if the **Edit Selected Paths** option is selected.

Brush Libraries

A **Brush Library** is a collection of preset brushes that you can select from to apply to illustrations. You can open brush libraries and add brushes from them to the **Brushes** panel. You can also create your own brush libraries and add brushes from other libraries or custom brushes to them.

The Brushes Panel

The *Brushes panel* displays the available brushes that you can apply to illustrations. If you select a brush from a brush library, that brush is added to the **Brushes** panel. You can create new brushes and manage them by using the options in the **Brushes** panel. Illustrator associates brushes, which you create and store in the **Brushes** panel, only with the current document.

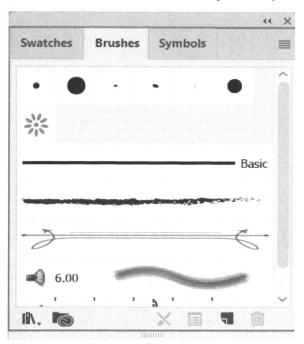

Figure 2-9: Pre-defined brushes displayed in the Brushes panel.

Brush Options

Brush options help you control the settings of a brush. Different brush types have different brush options that determine the size, colorization, and direction of the brushes. The scatter, art, and pattern brushes have the same options for colorization. Some of the brush options that are common to most of the types of brushes are spacing, rotation, colorization, and direction.

Brushes Modification

Illustrator has some very cool brush modification features. You can use raster graphics like JPEG, PNG, TIFF, or PSD files to create brushes. Make sure that the raster image is embedded in your document. You can then save the raster image as an **Art** brush, a **Pattern** brush, or a **Scatter** brush. After applying an image brush to your path, you can adjust its elements by changing the stroke width.

You can now also automatically create a corner tile for a **Pattern** brush. In the **Pattern Brush Options** dialog box, choose one of four types of corner tiles in the pop-up menu.

 Access the Checklist tile on your CHOICE Course screen for reference information and job aids on How to Paint with Custom Brushes.

ACTIVITY 2-3
Painting with Custom Brushes

Before You Begin

The My Emerald Epicure.ai file is open.

Scenario

You want to enhance the background of the third page of your brochure. You have created a flower and you want to scatter this flower along a path.

1. Create a brush.

   a) Unlock the **Seeds** layer in the **Layers** panel.
   b) At the top-right corner of artboard 2, select the flower on the right.

   c) On the **Application** bar, select **Windows→Brushes** to open the **Brushes** panel.
   d) In the **Brushes** panel, select the **New Brush** button.

   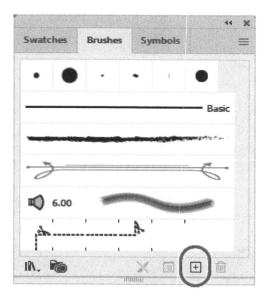

   e) In the **New Brush** dialog box, select **Scatter Brush** and select **OK**.
      If the flower isn't selected, the **Scatter Brush** option is dimmed.

2. Specify options for the **Scatter** brush.

   a) In the **Scatter Brush Options** dialog box, in the **Name** text box, enter *Green Flower*
   b) In the **Size** section, on the left slider, move the slider to **60%**.
   c) In the **Scatter** section, on the left slider, move the slider to **40%**.

d) In the **Rotation** section, on the left slider, move the slider to **20°** and select **OK**.

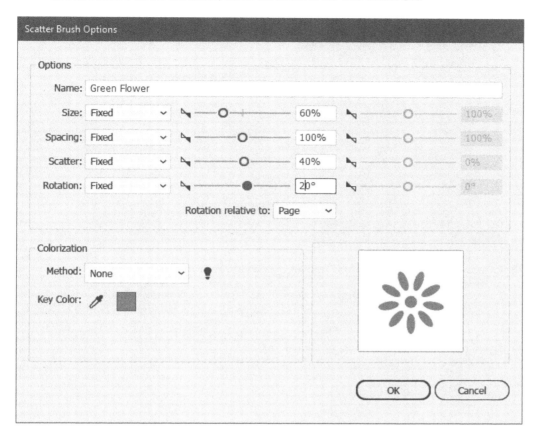

e) In the **Brushes** panel, observe that the brush is added to the set of brushes in the second row.

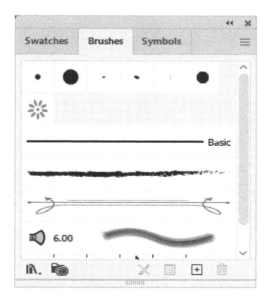

3. Draw a path by using the custom brush.

a) On the artboard, click anywhere outside the flower to deselect it.

b) In the **Brushes** panel, select the **Green Flower** brush.

c) In the **Tools** panel, select the **Paintbrush** tool.

d) On the artboard, drag to create an arc on the lower portion of artboard 2, as pictured in the following.

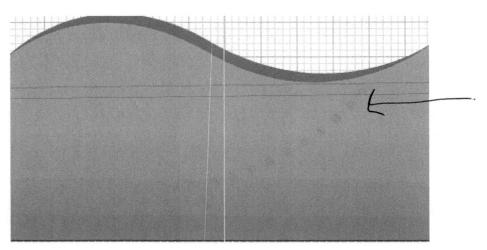

e) Observe that the green flower is scattered along the path you drew.

 Note: The green flowers are just slightly darker than the green background so they are difficult to see in the printed book; however, you should be able to see them on screen.

f) Save the file and leave it open for the next activity.

TOPIC D

Add Transparency and Blending Modes

You painted your artwork by using different techniques. As a designer, you will frequently come across situations in which you need to paint artwork so that you can see through objects to view underlying objects. Creating objects that are transparent and blending them with other objects will enhance your illustrations and add to their appeal. In this topic, you will apply transparency and blending modes.

Opacity

Opacity is a property of objects that can be set to create transparency so that you can see through objects to view other underlying objects. You can change the opacity of an object, a group of objects, or a layer. You can set opacity for objects in the **Transparency** panel.

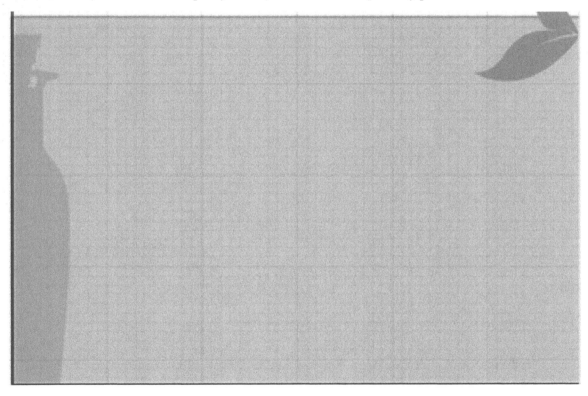

Figure 2–10: Opacity.

Opacity Masks

Transparency can be created in several different ways in Adobe illustrator. One of these ways is by using an *opacity mask*. What the mask does is create an area that is transparent over an object, with varying levels of transparency. In the space where the opacity mask is white, the layer beneath is shown. In the space where the mask is black, you cannot see the artwork below.

To create an opacity mask, select the desired items and then open the **Transparency** panel. From the **Panel Menu** select **Show Options**. By double-clicking the right thumbnail in the **Transparency** panel, you automatically create an empty mask, and are in mask-editing mode. Then, simply draw the desired mask shape by using any drawing tools.

Blending Modes

A *blending mode* determines the way colors of an object blend with the colors of the objects in the layers beneath it. The blend color is the color of the selected object and the base color is the color of the object in the underlying layer. The color resulting from the blend is called the resulting color. There are several blending modes that enable you to control the way colors blend. You can change the blending mode of an object by using the **Transparency** panel.

Transparency Panel

The **Transparency** panel is a convenient way to dictate opacity and blending modes, as well as create and edit opacity. In the **Transparency** panel, you can select a blending mode from the drop-down menu. You can also set an opacity level.

Figure 2–11: Transparency panel.

 Access the Checklist tile on your CHOICE Course screen for reference information and job aids on How to Add Transparency and Blending Modes.

ACTIVITY 2-4
Adding Transparency and Blending Modes

Before You Begin
My Emerald Epicure.ai is open.

Scenario
The traced image of the jar at the back cover of your brochure is very dark. You want to enhance the appearance of this image by making it look like the shadow of a bottle.

1. Create a background for the lower half of the brochure's back cover.
   a) Select artboard 1 on the left.
   b) Display the **Layers** panel.
   c) In the **Layers** panel, unlock and select **Layer 1**.
   d) Observe the brochure's back cover that contains the traced image of a jar.

      It is at the far left edge of artboard 1.
   e) Create a rectangle with a width of *6* inches and a height of *4* inches.
   f) Position the rectangle at the bottom of the artboard so that it covers the lower half of the brochure's back cover.
   g) Display the **Swatches** panel.
   h) Fill the rectangle with the third color in the second row of the **Swatches** panel.

   i) Right-click the rectangle and select **Arrange→Send to Back** to stack the rectangle behind the jar.

2. Change the blending mode of the jar.
   a) Select the jar.
   b) Display the **Transparency** panel.
   c) In the **Transparency** panel, from the **Blending Mode** drop-down list, select **Soft Light**.

d) Observe that the background color blends with the color of the jar.

3. Set the opacity of the jar and background.
   a) In the **Transparency** panel, select the **Opacity** drop-down arrow and move the slider to **50%**.
   b) In the artboard, observe that the jar has darkened a bit.
   c) Select the rectangle.
   d) In the **Transparency** panel, select the **Opacity** drop-down arrow and move the slider to **70%**.

   e) Observe that the rectangle is transparent, revealing the contents behind it.
   f) Save the file and leave it open for the next activity.

TOPIC E

Apply Meshes to Objects

You set the opacity and blending modes for objects to enhance your illustrations. Another technique to enhance illustrations is to apply multiple colors on an object in such a way that the colors transition smoothly. You can do this by using meshes. In this topic, you will apply meshes to objects.

Meshes

A *mesh* is a grid of lines that controls the flow and transition of colors across an object. The intersections of mesh lines contain special diamond-shaped anchor points called mesh points. You can add, edit, delete, and assign colors to mesh points. An area enclosed by a set of four mesh points is called a patch. As with mesh points, you can apply color to mesh patches as well. By moving the mesh points, you can control the color shift and change the size of a mesh patch.

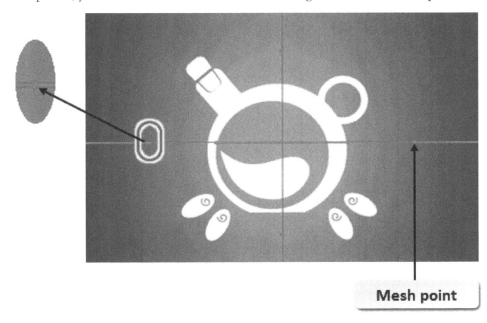

Mesh point

Figure 2–12: A mesh applied to the background of an image.

The Mesh Tool

You can use the **Mesh** tool to create a mesh with a random pattern of mesh points. To create a mesh with a regular pattern of mesh points, you can use the **Create Gradient Mesh** command.

Expand Function

The **Expand** function is available for many different Illustrator attributes. When it is used in a **Gradient Mesh**, it expands gradients to a single mesh object.

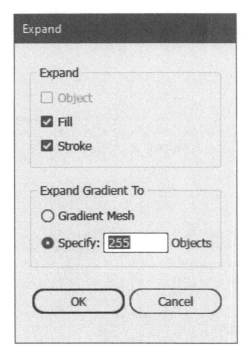

Figure 2-13: Expand function dialog box.

Gradient Mesh Transparency

Transparency can be set for a gradient mesh by altering the opacity values. To assign transparency values to a gradient mesh, select a mesh node or patch. Then from the **Transparency** panel, **Control** panel, or the **Appearance** panel, set the desired opacity level.

 Access the Checklist tile on your CHOICE Course screen for reference information and job aids on How to Apply Meshes to Objects.

ACTIVITY 2-5
Applying Meshes to an Object

Before You Begin

My Emerald Epicure.ai is open.

Scenario

You have created all the necessary objects for the front cover of your brochure. However, the background color is not appealing. You want to enhance the appearance of the background by transitioning multiple colors across it.

---

1. Fill and stroke the oil bottle and decorative elements on the page.

   a) Select all the components of the oil bottle.

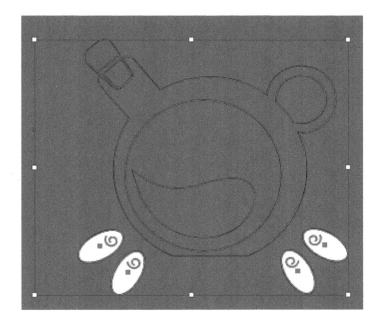

   Note: If you have trouble selecting the oil bottle components without also selecting the rectangle behind it, in the **Layers** panel, hide **Page 2 Background** by clicking the **Eye** icon.

   b) In the **Tools** panel, select the **Fill** button and in the **Swatches** panel, select a white color to apply white to the selected components.

c) In the **Tools** panel, select the **Stroke** button, and then select **[None]** to remove the black stroke.

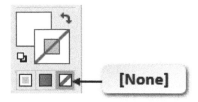

Make sure you have applied a white fill and no stroke color.

2. Create a mesh for the background of the page.

   a) In the **Layers** panel, select the **Page 1 Background** layer.
   b) In the **Tools** panel, verify the **Selection** tool is selected.
   c) On the artboard, select the green rectangle behind the oil bottle.
   d) In the **Tools** panel, select the **Fill** button.

   e) In the **Tools** panel, select the **Mesh** tool.

f)   Select the center of the rectangle.

g)   Observe that a mesh dividing the rectangle into four is displayed.

3. Apply colors to the mesh.

a)   In the **Swatches** panel, select the third color (green) in the second row.

b) Observe that the mesh shows a transition between two shades of green.

c) In the **Tools** panel, select the **Selection** tool.
d) On the artboard, click an empty area away from the rectangle.
e) Save the file and leave it open for the next activity.

TOPIC F

Apply Patterns

You painted objects with multiple colors by using meshes. Consider a situation in which you need to paint an object with a repeating flowery design. You can do this by creating a flower pattern and applying it to your object. In this topic, you will apply patterns to objects.

Patterns

A *pattern* is a repeatable shape that you can use to fill objects or stroke a path. A fill pattern fills objects and a brush pattern strokes the outlines of objects. You can either use pre-defined patterns that are available in the **Swatches** panel or create custom patterns.

Object filled using the pattern.

Figure 2–14: A pattern used to fill an object.

Pattern Tiles

While applying a pattern, Illustrator creates multiple instances of that pattern. These instances are called pattern tiles. Pattern tiles are arranged from left to right starting from the ruler origin. Fill patterns tile perpendicular to the X axis, and brush patterns tile perpendicular to the path.

The Pattern Options Panel

The **Pattern Options** panel provides options that enable you to design patterns.

Option	Description
Name	Defines the pattern's name.
Tile Type	Specifies the tile type of the pattern. Tile type can be **Grid**, **Brick by Row**, **Brick by Column**, **Hex by Row**, and **Hex by Column**.
Brick Offset	Amount by which tile centers are out of alignment with adjacent tiles.
Width	Sets the width of a pattern tile.
Height	Sets the height of a pattern tile.
Size Tile to Art	Determines whether the size of the pattern is controlled by the size of the artwork.

Option	Description
Move Tile with Art	Determines whether the pattern tiles move when the artwork moves.
H Spacing and V Spacing	Distance between adjacent tiles.
Overlap	Specifies the way pattern tiles overlap.
Copies	Sets the number of pattern tile copies.
Dim Copies to	Sets the brightness level of the copies.
Show Tile Edge	Determines whether or not pattern tile edges are visible.
Show Swatch Bounds	Determines whether or not the swatch bounds are visible.

 Note: To learn more about applying patterns, check out the LearnTO **Create Patterns** presentation from the **LearnTO** tile on the CHOICE Course screen.

Tile Edge Transformation

Changing the edge color of a pattern tile can have interesting effects, as long as you don't want the desired look to appear seamless. Access the pattern options by double-clicking the pattern in the **Swatch** panel. Select the **Pattern options** menu and then select **Tile Edge Color**. From the pattern tile edge color dialog box, you can choose from the list of options or double-click the **Color** button and choose a custom color.

Pattern Fills

Illustrator has many patterns that you can select from in the **Swatches** panel. You can customize existing patterns and design patterns from scratch by using any of the Illustrator tools. When selecting patterns, use fill patterns to fill objects and brush patterns to outline objects. Patterns that are intended to fill objects differ in design and tiling from patterns intended to be applied to a path:

- Fill patterns typically have only one tile.
- Fill patterns tile perpendicular to the x axis.
- Fill patterns only tile artwork within the pattern bounding box.
- With fill patterns, the bounding box acts as a mask.

 Access the Checklist tile on your CHOICE Course screen for reference information and job aids on How to Apply Patterns.

ACTIVITY 2-6
Applying Patterns

Before You Begin

My Emerald Epicure.ai is open.

If you hid **Page 2 Background** previously, unhide it now.

Scenario

The bottom portion of the last page of the brochure does not look too interesting with just the image of the jar. You want to make this page more appealing by adding a flowery border to the bottom.

---

1. Create a pattern from a flower shape.
   a) Select artboard 2.
   b) In the **Tools** panel, select the **Selection** tool.
   c) On the artboard, draw a rectangular marquee around the left flower shaped object.

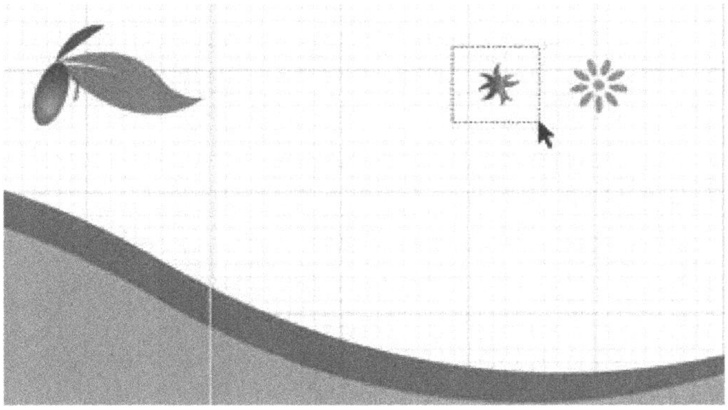

Hold down space bar to pan

   d) Select **Object→Pattern→Make** to create a pattern out of the selected object.
   e) In the **Adobe Illustrator** message box, a message is displayed indicating that the new pattern has been added to the **Swatches** panel. Select **OK**.

f) In the **Swatches** panel, observe that the pattern you created is added in the fourth row. (You might need to scroll the swatches to see it,)

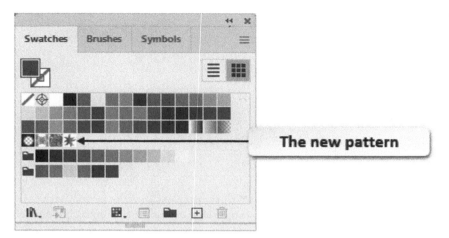

The new pattern

2. Set options for the new pattern.

a) In the **Pattern Options** panel, in the **Name** text box, replace "New Pattern" with *Flower Pattern*
b) From the **Tile Type** drop-down list, select **Hex by Row**.
c) Check the **Size Tile to Art** check box.
d) From the **Copies** drop-down list, select **5 x 3**.

e) Observe that the pattern is updated based on the changes you made in the **Pattern Options** panel.

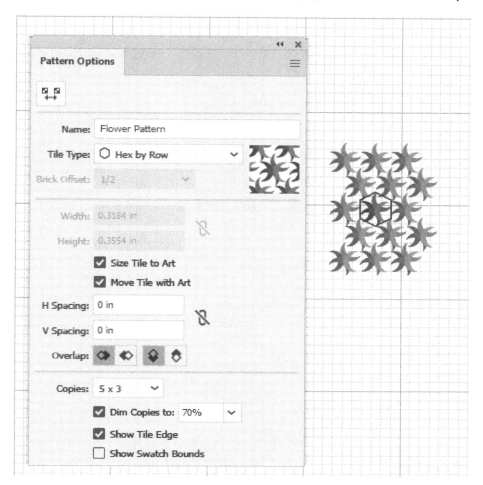

f) Above the artboard, in the gray color bar, select **Done**.

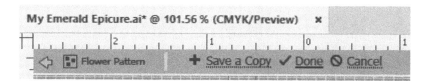

3. Create a border for the bottom of the last page of your brochure.

   a) Scroll to view the bottom-left corner of artboard 1.
   b) In the **Layers** panel, select **Layer 1**.
   c) Select **White** as the current fill color and set the stroke color as **None**.

d) Create a rectangle with a width of **6** inches and a height of **0.3** inches. Move the rectangle and position it so that the bottom edge of the rectangle touches the bottom border of the artboard.

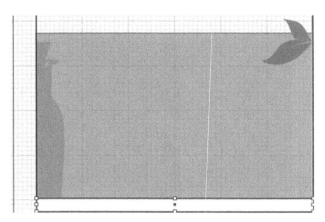

4. Apply the new pattern to the rectangle

a) In the **Tools** panel, select the **Fill** button.
b) In the **Swatches** panel, select the **Flower Pattern** swatch.
c) Observe that the rectangle is filled with the flower pattern .

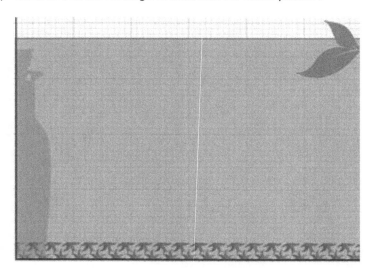

5. Save and close the file.

Summary

In this lesson, you used painting tools to enhance artwork. You can now control the way your objects are filled and stroked and enhance their appearance by using multiple colors, gradients, and patterns.

Suppose you need to fill the objects in your artwork with multiple colors. Which tools would you use to complete this task? Why?

Give examples of when you would choose to use a custom brush or patterns to paint objects.

 Note: Check your CHOICE Course screen for opportunities to interact with your classmates, peers, and the larger CHOICE online community about the topics covered in this course or other topics you are interested in. From the Course screen you can also access available resources for a more continuous learning experience.

3 Customizing Colors and Swatches

Lesson Time: 45 minutes

Lesson Introduction

You have used painting tools to enhance artwork. Imagine a situation in which you need to apply natural looking colors to an object. You may not be able to achieve the desired outcome by using the default swatches and colors available in Adobe® Illustrator®. However, you can customize the default colors and swatches to paint objects according to your preference. In this lesson, you will customize colors and swatches.

Lesson Objectives

In this lesson, you will:

*   Manage colors.

*   Customize swatches.

*   Manage color groups.

*   Adjust color.

TOPIC A

Manage Colors

You painted objects by using different techniques. You can make sure that the objects are painted with perfect colors by either editing colors or by selecting a required color from a swatch. In this topic, you will manage colors.

Color Models

Color models define how a range of colors are produced based on a few colors. They use combinations of the base colors represented as numerical values to generate a spectrum of colors. A range of colors generated by a color model reproduced under specified conditions is called a color space. Each color space in a color model supports a unique range of colors in the visible spectrum. The range of colors that a color space supports is called a gamut. There are four commonly used color models plus grayscale.

Color Model	Description
RGB	Uses Red, Green, and Blue as the base colors and derives other colors by mixing these colors. By assigning a value between 0 and 255 to each component in RGB, you can create a range of colors. This model is suitable for reproducing colors on television and computer monitors.
CMYK	Uses Cyan, Magenta, Yellow, and Black as the base colors. Black color adds shadow density. Each of the four colors in CMYK takes a value between 0 and 100 percent to produce other colors. The CMYK model is suitable for printing documents and the four colors are called process inks.
HSB	Describes a color by using the Hue, Saturation, and Brightness characteristics. Hue is the color reflected or transmitted through an object. Saturation is the purity of the color. Brightness represents the percentage of lightness or darkness of the color.
Lab	Describes the colors perceived by the human eye in the form of numerical values. It is a device-independent color model.
Grayscale	Uses Black tints with varying brightness values. A brightness value of 100% produces black and a value of 0% produces white. Values in between are various shades of gray. This can be used to convert a color artwork to a black and white artwork.

Default is CMYK

Color Modes in Illustrator

Illustrator supports the RGB and CMYK color models. You can create documents based on one of these two color modes. The RGB color mode is suitable for creating artwork for the web, and the CMYK color mode is suitable for printing artwork.

Grayscale Images

Grayscale images are reproduced in black, white, and shades of gray. The color value can range from 0 percent (white) to 100 percent (black). Values between these percentages are shades of gray.

Global Colors

In Illustrator, a global color is one that remains linked to a swatch. If you modify a swatch in the **Swatches** panel, all objects that use that color get updated. It's a quick and easy way to test various hues and moods in your artwork.

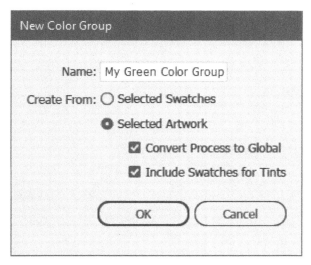

Figure 3-1: Convert colors to global colors in the New Color Group dialog box.

Output Color Types

When Illustrator artwork is printed, it can be reproduced by using one of two color types—process colors or spot colors.

Color Type	Description
Process Color	Uses a combination of the CMYK inks to display color. Process colors are less expensive and are best suited for printing color-intensive artwork.
Spot Color	Uses a single ink to display color. Spot colors replicate colors accurately and consistently. They are used to reproduce colors that are not available in the gamut of the CMYK color model.

The Color Panel

The **Color** panel provides a color spectrum and color sliders for selecting fill and stroke colors. You can also specify colors by setting numerical values for the base colors in the currently selected color mode. The **Color** panel does not show the individual CMYK values by default. In order to see them in the **Color** panel, from the panel menu, select **Show Options**.

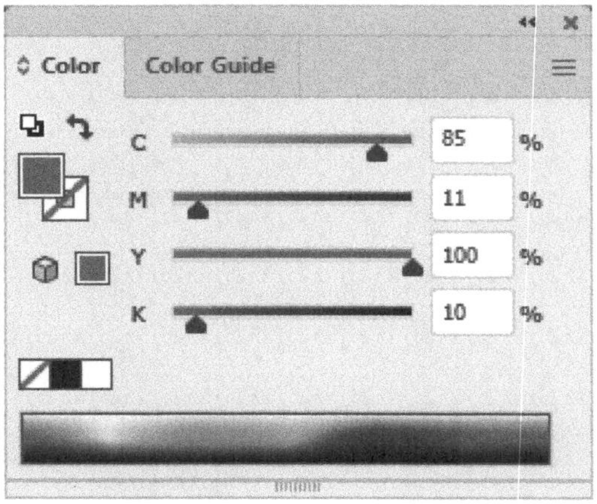

Figure 3–2: The Color panel displaying the CMYK values for the selected color.

Access the Checklist tile on your CHOICE Course screen for reference information and job aids on How to Manage Colors.

ACTIVITY 3–1
Managing Colors in Artwork

Data File

C:\092034Data\Customizing Colors and Swatches\Emerald Epicure.ai

Scenario

You want to add a natural-looking color to the background on the last page of your brochure. However, the colors available in the **Swatches** panel do not appeal to you. You want to look for some other natural-looking color that will suit your brochure.

1. Open **C:\092034Data\Customizing Colors and Swatches\Emerald Epicure.ai**.

2. Select the background of the left artboard that has to be filled with a natural-looking color.

   a) Select artboard **1** and select **Fit On Screen**.
   b) Select the **Selection** tool.
   c) In the **Layers** panel, select **Layer 1**.
   d) Select the rectangle that forms a transparent background for the jar.

3. Access swatches from the **Fruit** swatch library.

   a) In the **Swatches** panel, at the bottom of the panel, select the **Swatch Libraries** menu button.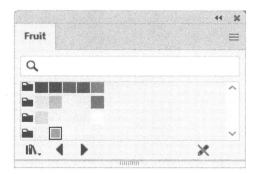
   b) From the menu that appears, select **Foods→Fruit**.
   c) Observe that the **Fruit** swatch library is displayed in a **Fruit** panel, separate from the **Swatches** panel.

   d) Resize the **Fruit** panel to view the entire set of color groups in the **Fruit** swatch library.
   e) In the **Tools** panel, select the **Fill** button.

f) From the colors in the **Fruit** panel, select the first color swatch in the twelfth row. It is a light green, the first color in the all green group.

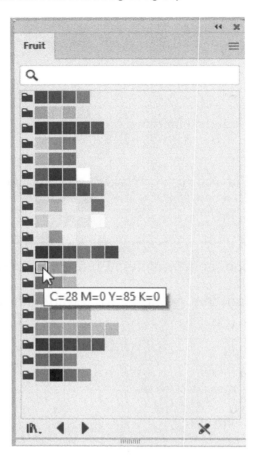

g) Observe that the rectangle is filled with the color selected in the **Fruit** panel.

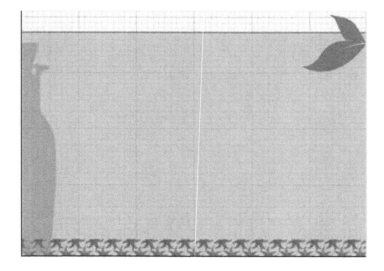

4. Move the selected color swatch from the **Fruit** swatch library to the **Swatches** panel.

a) In the **Fruit** panel, from the panel menu, select **Add to Swatches** to move the selected color to the **Swatches** panel.

b) In the **Swatches** panel, observe that the color swatch you selected is added at the end of the fourth row.

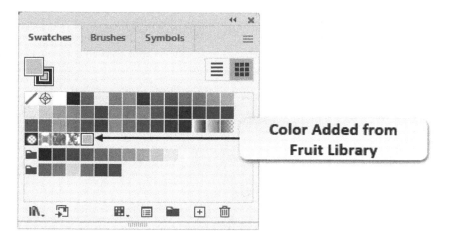

Color Added from
Fruit Library

c) Close the **Fruit** panel.

5. Edit the color in the **Color** panel.

a) In the **Color** panel, from the panel menu, select **Show Options**.

If options are already displayed, the panel menu shows **Hide Options** instead.

b) Observe that the **Color** panel shows sliders and text boxes that you can use to specify the intensity of each component in the current color mode.

c) If the sliders are not labeled CMYK, from the panel menu, select **CMYK**.

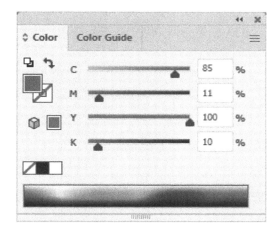

d) In the **C** text box, enter *20*

e) Verify that the **M** and **K** text boxes are set to **0%**.

f) In the **Y** text box, enter *100* and press **Enter**.

g) Observe that the selected rectangle is updated with the changed color.

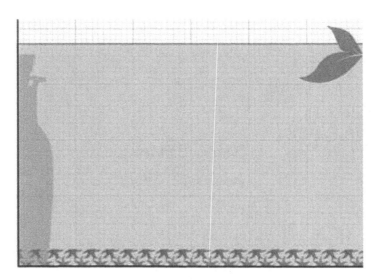

h) On the artboard, click the white space above the rectangle to deselect it.
i) Select **File→Save As**.
j) Navigate to the **C:\092034Data\Customizing Colors and Swatches** folder and save the file as *My Emerald Epicure.ai*
k) In the **Illustrator Options** dialog box, select **OK** to accept the default settings.
l) Leave the file open for the next activity.

TOPIC B

Customize Swatches

You managed colors and swatches in your document. Though a wide variety of swatches are available in the different swatch libraries, you may still need to customize a swatch to suit your needs. In this topic, you will customize swatches.

Swatches

A *swatch* is a named color, gradient, or pattern that you can use to fill and stroke objects. The **Swatches** panel displays the swatches associated with the current document. You can view the swatches in the **Swatches** panel in thumbnail or list view.

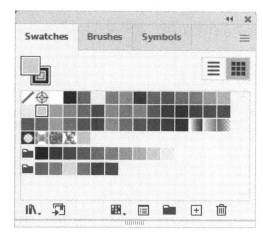

Figure 3–3: A collection of swatches in the Swatches panel.

Types of Swatches

The **Swatches** panel displays different types of swatches such as process color swatches, spot color swatches, gradient swatches, pattern swatches, and color groups. The **Swatches** panel indicates the type of swatches displayed when you view the swatches in list view.

Swatch Libraries

A swatch library is a collection of preset swatches. Swatch libraries include color books, such as Pantone, HSK, TRUMATCH, and FOCOLTONE, and collections of thematic swatches, such as **Nature**, **Textiles**, **Corporate**, **Kids Stuff**, and **Neutral**. Swatch libraries open in a separate panel of their own. Because swatch libraries are pre-defined collections, you cannot add, edit, or delete the swatches in a swatch library.

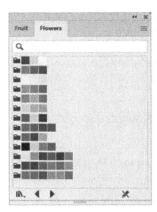

Figure 3–4: Swatches in the Flowers swatch library.

Shared Swatches

Once a swatch has been created, it can also be shared between Adobe applications such as Adobe Photoshop® and Adobe InDesign®. As long as the swatches are solid they will appear if the color settings are synchronized. In order to share swatches, go to the **Swatches** panel and remove any swatches you do not wish to share. From the **Swatches** panel menu, select **Save Swatch Library as ASE**. Make sure you choose a convenient location in which to save the swatch library. In the other program, load the swatch library into the **Swatches** panel.

Swatch Options

Swatch options are settings that control a swatch. By setting swatch options, you can customize a swatch or create a new swatch.

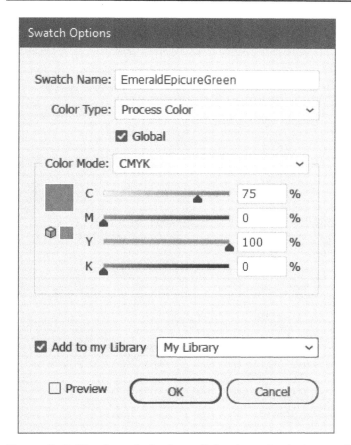

Figure 3–5: The Swatch Options dialog box displaying options to customize a swatch.

Swatch Option	Description
Swatch Name	Specifies the name of the swatch.
Color Type	Sets the type of color in the swatch. The default color type is Process Color.
Global	Makes the process color swatch available to the entire document so that when the swatch is edited, all objects that use the swatch are updated automatically. When you create a swatch, this option is selected by default.
Color Mode	Specifies the color mode for the swatch. Once you select a color mode, you can select the color for the swatch.
Add to my Library	Adds the swatch to a swatch library which you have created.
Preview	Displays a preview of the swatch.

 Note: To learn more about customizing swatches, check out the LearnTO **Create Custom Swatches** presentation from the **LearnTO** tile on the CHOICE Course screen.

 Access the Checklist tile on your CHOICE Course screen for reference information and job aids on How to Customize Swatches.

ACTIVITY 3–2
Customizing a Swatch

Before You Begin

My Emerald Epicure.ai is open.

Scenario

Now that you have a background for the bottom half of your last page, you want to apply a background color to the top half as well. Instead of choosing one of the preset swatches for your background, you want to define a color and create a new swatch with it.

---

1. Create a swatch.

    a) In the **Swatches** panel, make sure there is not a particular color selected, or it will be overwritten.

    Deselect any specific colors in the swatches panel and then select the **New Swatch** button. ⊞

    b) In the **New Swatch** dialog box, in the **Swatch Name** text box, type *My New Swatch* to replace the default swatch name.

    c) In the **Color Type** drop-down list, verify that **Process Color** is selected.

    d) Verify the **Global** check box is unchecked.

    e) In the **C** text box, enter *90.5*

    f) In the **M** text box, enter *38.5*

    g) In the **Y** text box, enter *98.5*

    h) In the **K** text box, enter *38.5*

i) Verify **Add to my Library** is unchecked, then select **OK**.

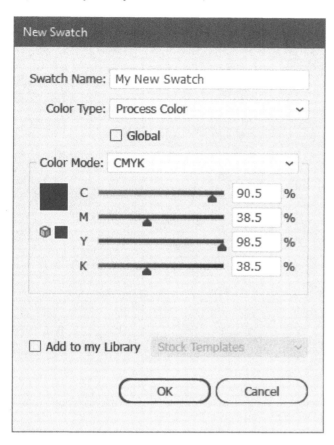

j) In the **Swatches** panel, observe that the swatch you created is added, and that it is currently selected.

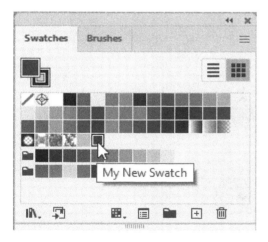

2. Create a background for the top half of the last page of the brochure.

a) In the **Layers** panel, select **Layer1**.

b) Create a rectangle with a width of **6** inches and a height of **4.24** inches.

c) Observe that the rectangle is filled with the color of the swatch you created.

d) Position the rectangle so that its center is at approximately **3** inches on the horizontal ruler and **2.1** inches on the vertical ruler and it covers the top half of the page.

e) Right-click the rectangle and select **Arrange→Send to Back**.

f) Click outside the margin of the artboard to deselect the rectangle.

g) Save the file and leave it open for the next activity.

TOPIC C

Manage Color Groups

You used custom swatches to apply color to objects. As you create more swatches, you may find it difficult to quickly find the right swatch for your artwork. You can quickly access the swatches that you require if you organize them into groups based on color. In this topic, you will manage color groups.

Color Groups

A *color group* is a group of related color swatches in the **Swatches** panel. Color groups help organize colors. You can create harmonious color groups by using the **Color Guide** panel and the **Edit Colors/Recolor Artwork** dialog box. Color groups can contain only solid colors and cannot have gradients and patterns.

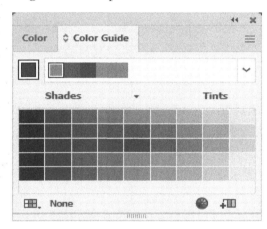

Figure 3-6: A color group displayed in the Color Guide panel.

The Color Guide and Color Themes Panels

The **Color Guide** panel helps you select appropriate colors by suggesting harmonious color combinations for your artwork. This panel uses color harmony rules to generate harmonious colors. You can edit the harmony rules and adjust the settings in the **Color Guide** panel to generate the colors you require.

The *Color Themes panel* enables you to create color themes or select a color theme created by professional graphic designers and shared online. You can also use these themes in Adobe Photoshop, Adobe InDesign, and Adobe After Effects..

Recolor Artwork

Illustrator's **Recolor Artwork** feature is a powerful tool that lets you quickly colorize or change the color of your artwork without having to change each vector image individually. It can be used for both illustration and graphic design, and gives you dramatic flexibility to experiment with color and quickly try new color schemes.

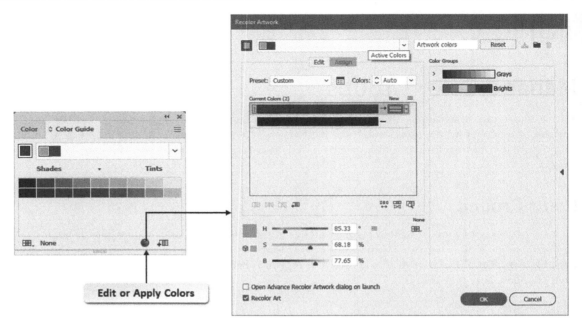

Figure 3-7: Select the Edit or Apply Colors button to open the Recolor Artwork dialog box.

Note: If an object is selected, the **Color Guide** panel has the **Edit or Apply Colors** button and the **Recolor Artwork** dialog box opens. If no objects are selected, the button becomes the **Edit Colors** button and the **Edit Colors** dialog box opens. The options on the **Edit Colors** dialog box are also available in the **Recolor Artwork** dialog box on the **Edit** tab.

Edit Colors Dialog Box

The **Edit Colors** dialog box offers an easy way to adjust colors that are already in a selected artwork. Colors can be added using the **Smooth color wheel**, the **Segmented color wheel**, or **Color bars**. The **Smooth color wheel** shows hue, saturation, and brightness within a seamless circle. Although you can choose from many different colors, it is difficult to get a precise color location. The **Segmented color wheel** shows sections of color patches. Although these sections are easy to choose with precision, there are not as many options as in the **Smooth color wheel**. And finally, **Color bars** show only colors that are within the color group.

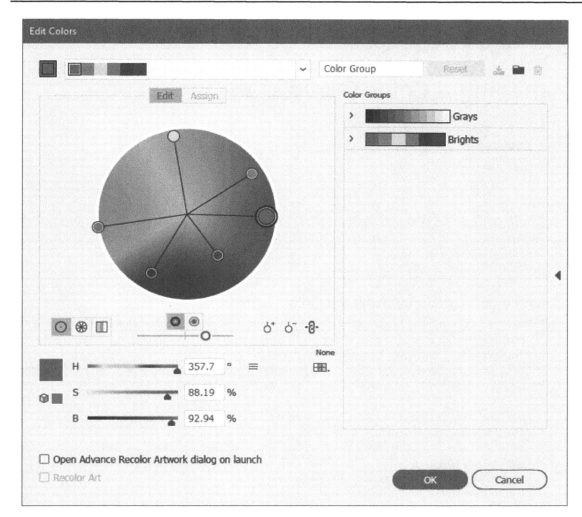

Figure 3-8: Edit Colors dialog box.

Color Sampling

Illustrator has a variety of tools you can use to select colors for your artwork. In many cases, you may wish to sample an existing color to match it exactly. If you want to match a color in some other artwork, you can use the **Eyedropper** tool to sample the color. You can also use the **Color Picker** to enter exact color values. The **Eyedropper** tool is located on the **Tools** panel.

 Access the Checklist tile on your CHOICE Course screen for reference information and job aids on How to Manage Color Groups.

ACTIVITY 3-3
Managing a Color Group

Before You Begin
My Emerald Epicure.ai file is open.

Scenario
As you continue to apply different colors to the brochure artwork, it becomes difficult to locate the colors you have used. To track all the colors you need, you would like to group them in a way that helps you access them easily.

---

1. Create a color group by using the **Color Guide** panel.

   a) Make sure that no objects are selected on the artboard. In the **Swatches** panel, if necessary, select **My New Swatch**.

   b) In the **Color** panel group, select the **Color Guide** panel.

   c) In the **Color Guide** panel, in the **Color** box to the left of the **Harmony Rules** drop-down list, verify that the color you selected in the **Swatches** panel is displayed as the base color for the Harmony Rules.

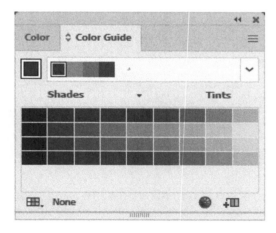

d) From the **Harmony Rules** drop-down list, select **Shades**.

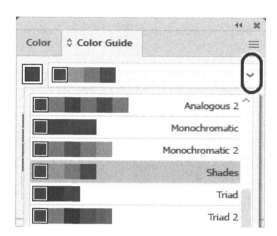

e) In the gallery of colors, select the third color in the second row.
f) Hold **Shift** and select the eighth color in the second row to select a set of colors.
g) Select the **Save color group to Swatch panel** button.

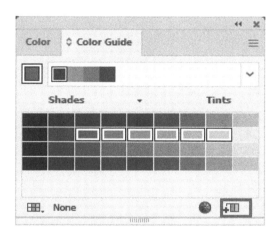

h) In the **Swatches** panel, observe that a new color group is added with the colors you selected in the **Color Guide** panel.

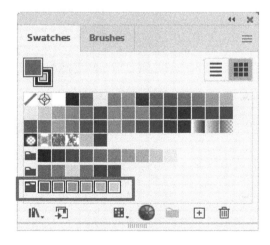

2. Edit the color group you created.

a) Make sure that the new color group is selected in the **Swatches** panel, and select the **Edit Color Group** button.

b) In the **Edit Colors** dialog box, in the text box to the right of the **Harmony Rules** drop-down list, replace "Color Group 1" with *My New Color Group*

c) In the left pane below the color wheel, select the **Display color bars** button.

d) In the set of color bars, select the third color from the left.

e) In the **H** text box, enter *140*

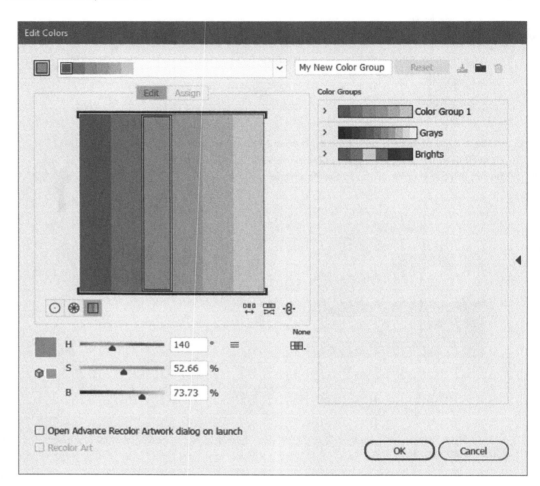

f) Select **OK**.

g) When prompted to save changes, select **Yes**.

h) In the **Swatches** panel, click anywhere outside the currently selected color group to deselect it.

i) Save and close the file.

TOPIC D

Adjust Color

You organized colors into color groups for quick access. Now you will learn advanced color management techniques such as blending, manipulation, and mixing. You will learn how to deal with colors that cannot be printed, and how to use spot colors and saturation. In this topic, you will adjust color.

Out-of-Gamut Color

An out-of-gamut color is one that has no similar color in the CMYK model. Because of this, the color cannot be printed. An example of an out-of-gamut color would be a neon color. When an out-of-gamut color is chosen, Illustrator alerts you with an alert triangle in the **Color** panel or **Color Picker**. When this occurs, you can easily shift to a safer, printable color.

Color Blending

Illustrator allows you to blend colors by using the **Blend** commands. When you do so, midrange objects are filled with a blend created from a group of three or more filled objects. In order to blend colors, you need to select three or more filled objects.

The objects can be filled with graduated blends from:

* Front to back
* Horizontally
* Vertically

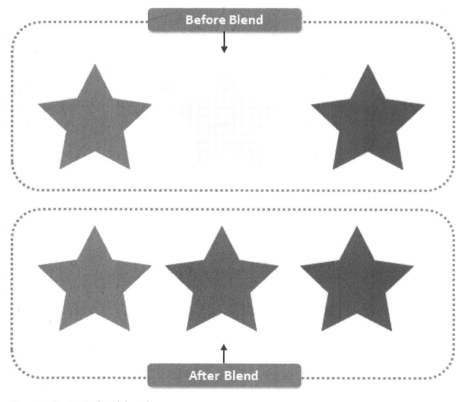

Figure 3-9: Color blending.

Color Manipulation

In Illustrator, color can be manipulated in many different ways. To change a color to its inverse or complement, from the **Color** panel menu, select **Invert**. This changes the color to its opposite value. You can also select **Complement**, which changes the color based on its color wheel complement. In addition, you can adjust color balance or saturation, or convert to grayscale.

Spot Colors

In some cases, you may have a specialty print in which you want to showcase a specific color. Although spot color inks produce accurate results of a color that is not a normal CMYK model color, it requires its own printing plate on a printing press. When determining the specifications of the spot color, you also need to consider the printer and paper that is being used. It is best to use a color matching system that is provided in Illustrator. If possible, minimize the number of spot colors that you use in order to keep printing costs down.

Saturation

Saturation is a color-editing feature that enables you to alter an object's vividness or brightness. Changing an object's saturation changes the object's color intensity. It causes it to appear more vibrant or less intense. Increasing saturation values creates the impression of a high-tech-looking color. Lowering saturation values often gives a color an earthy feel. Increase a color's saturation to achieve a brighter, richer color. Decrease saturation to lessen a color's vibrancy and brightness.

Color Mixing

Sometimes choosing a swatch from the **Swatches** panel does not provide the ideal color for the artwork. In this case, you can use the **Color** panel to easily change the color of the swatch by using the **CMYK** or **RGB** sliders. When you do this, you are simply adding more or less of the specified color. Values that appear next to the sliders create a new color that is specified by the percentages of cyan, magenta, yellow, and black, or red, green, and blue.

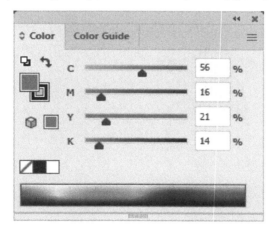

Figure 3–10: Color mixing.

 Access the Checklist tile on your CHOICE Course screen for reference information and job aids on How to Adjust Color.

ACTIVITY 3-4
Adjusting Color

Scenario

The Emerald Epicure marketing team is considering adding color effects to their new series of flyers. They want to better understand the effect of blending and manipulating colors. They have asked you to demonstrate to their team creating color blends, inverses, and complements.

1. Create a new document in Illustrator.

   a) From the **Start** workspace, select the **Create New** button.
   b) Select **More Settings**.
   c) In the **More Settings** dialog box, in the **Name** box, type *Color Manipulation Demo*
   d) Configure the settings as shown in the image.

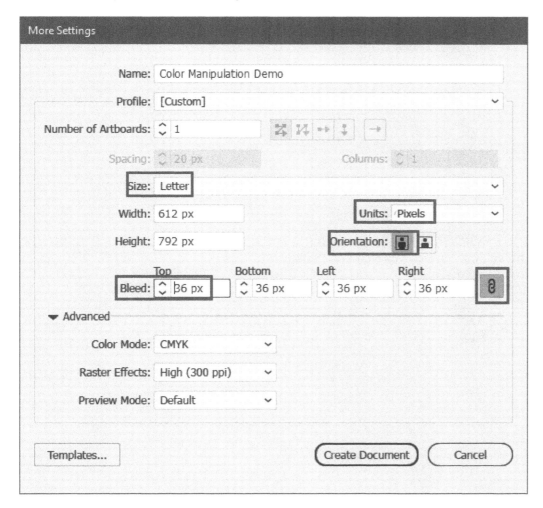

   e) Select **Create Document**.

2. Create nine five-pointed stars.

a) In the **Tools** panel, select the **Rectangle** tool, and from the menu, select the **Star** tool.

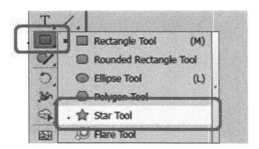

b) Click in the upper-left corner of the blank document to open the **Star** dialog box.
c) In the **Star** dialog box, in the **Radius 1** field, enter *44 px*
d) In the **Radius 2** field, enter *22 px*
e) Verify that the **Points** field value is **5**.

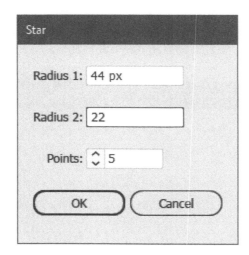

f) Select **OK**.

3. Add color to the star.

a) Verify that the star you drew is still selected.
b) In the **Tools** panel, double-click the **Fill** button to open the **Color Picker**.

c) In the **Color Picker** dialog box, in the **#** text box, type *18F906* then press **Tab** and select **OK**.

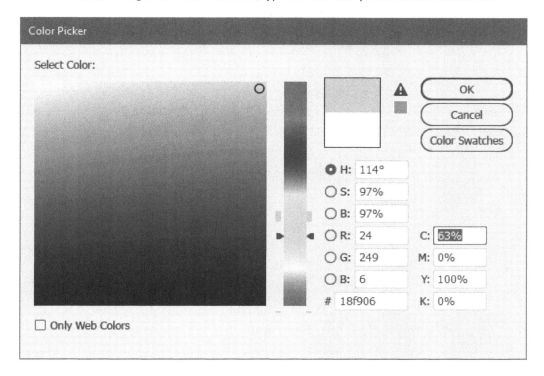

d) Verify that the **Stroke** is set to **black**. The star on the artboard turns to green with a black outline.

4. Make eight copies of the star.

a) Use the **Selection** tool to select the star.

b) With the star selected, hold the **Alt** key and drag to the right to create a copy of the star.

c) Hold the **Alt** key and drag again to create a third star.

You can use the Smart Guides to align the new stars but you don't need to be precise.

d) Deselect the third star.

e) Click a bit to the left and above the left star and drag down and to the right to select all three stars.

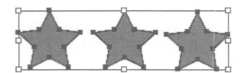

f) Select one of the stars, and holding down the **Alt** key drag down to create a copy of the three stars.
g) Drag down one more time to create a third row of stars.

5. Change the right column of stars to red.
    a) Press and hold **Shift** as you select each star in the right column of stars.
    b) In the **Tools** panel, double-click the **Fill** button to open the **Color Picker**.
    c) In the **Color Picker**, move the slider to the top of the red area, and then select the top-right corner of the color palette to select the red color.

       Alternatively, you can enter *F70B16* in the text box.
    d) Select **OK**. The right column of stars turns red.

6. Blend the colors.
    a) Select the top three stars.
    b) On the **Application** bar, select **Edit→Edit Colors→Blend Front to Back**.

c) Verify that the color of the top middle star is a blend of the left and right stars.

d) Select the top six stars.
e) Select **Edit→Edit Colors→Blend Horizontally**.
f) Verify that all six stars are a different blend of green and red, using colors from the left and right stars.

g) Select the middle row of stars.
h) Select **Edit→Edit Colors→Blend Vertically**.
i) Verify that the stars have a new blend of colors taken from the top and bottom stars.

7. Manipulate colors with Inverse and Complements.

a) Select the bottom-left star.

b) If necessary, display the **Color** panel.

c) In the **Color** panel, select the panel menu.

d) Select **RGB**.

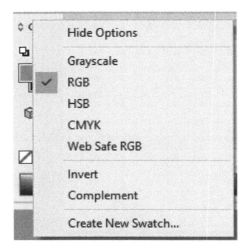

e) In the **Color** panel, verify that the hexadecimal number for the color is **#68BD45**.

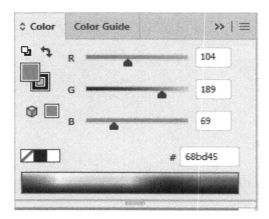

f) From the panel menu, select **Invert**.

g) Verify that the star color has changed to its inverse **#9642B9**.

h) Select the bottom-middle star.

i) In the **Color** panel, verify that the color is **#68BD45**.

j) In the **Color** panel, from the panel menu, select **Complement**.

k) Verify that the color has become its complement, **#9A45BD**.

Note: **Invert** and **Complement** will produce results that look very similar but are not really the same. **Invert** changes each component of a color to its opposite on the color scale. For example, if an RGB color has an R value of 50, the **Invert** command will change the R value to 205 (255 – 50 = 205). **Complement** changes each component of a color to a new color. The new color will be the sum of the highest and lowest RGB values. For example, if you have a color with an RGB value of 50 for red, 100 for green, and 25 for blue, Illustrator will add the high (100) and low (25), to end up with a new value of 125.

8. Are the results of the Invert and the Complement commands exactly the same?

9. Save the file in the folder C:\092034Data\Customizing Colors and Swatches as *My Color Manipulation Demo.ai*

10. In the **Illustrator Options** dialog box, select **OK** to accept the default settings.

11. Close the file.

Summary

In this lesson, you customized colors and swatches. You can now organize the colors and swatches you use in a document and create new swatches for your artwork.

Suppose you are working on illustrations for a series of children's books. How will you choose colors for your illustrations and keep the colors easily accessible?

Provide instances of when you would create a color group.

Note: Check your CHOICE Course screen for opportunities to interact with your classmates, peers, and the larger CHOICE online community about the topics covered in this course or other topics you are interested in. From the Course screen you can also access available resources for a more continuous learning experience.

4 Formatting Type

Lesson Time: 30 minutes

Lesson Introduction

You controlled the way colors and swatches affect your illustrations. Controlling the appearance of text is also equally important, if you want your artwork to look great. Whether you have short titles and sentences or large blocks of text, you need to enhance the appearance of the text in your artwork. In this lesson, you will format type.

Lesson Objectives

In this lesson, you will:

• Set character formats.

• Apply advanced formatting options to type.

TOPIC A

Set Character Formats

You organized colors and swatches to gain control over the appearance of your artwork. Another important element in your artwork is text. Managing the type in your document will not only allow you to present information effectively, but will also add to the visual appeal of your artwork. In this topic, you will enhance the appearance of text by setting character formats.

Basic Character Formats

Basic character formats define formatting and spacing options you can apply to text.

Figure 4-1: The Character panel displaying options to set basic character formatting settings.

The following table lists six basic character formats available.

Basic Character Formats	Description
Font Family	A collection of fonts that have common characteristics resulting in similarity in appearance.
Font Style	A variant of an individual font in a font family, such as regular, bold, italic, and bold italic styles.
Font Size	The size of text.
Leading	The vertical space between one line of text and the line below it.
Kerning	The amount of space to be added or reduced between a pair of characters.
Tracking	The extent to which the space between a set of characters is tightened or loosened.

Fractional Character Widths

By default, the character spacing among characters in type varies. This is because the spacing may be a fraction of a pixel. Fractional character widths enhance the readability and appearance of type, but they may cause the characters to overlap if the font size is very small. You can turn fractional character widths off if you do not want type to have fractional spacing variations.

Missing Fonts

When you open a document that contains fonts that are not installed on your system, an alert message identifies which fonts are missing and uses available matching fonts to substitute for the missing fonts. You can then decide if you want to accept the suggested substitute fonts, install or activate the missing fonts, or use different substitute fonts.

You can configure Illustrator to **Auto-activate Adobe Fonts** in **Preferences** dialog box on the **File Handling** tab. If all of the missing fonts are Adobe Fonts, they will automatically be activated in the background. If all or some of the missing fonts are from a source other than Adobe Fonts, you will be prompted on how you want to handle those fonts.

Advanced Character Formats

Advanced character formats define the way characters are transformed. By using advanced character formats, you can scale, rotate, and shift the baseline of characters, change case, add subscripts and superscripts, and apply underlines and strikethroughs.

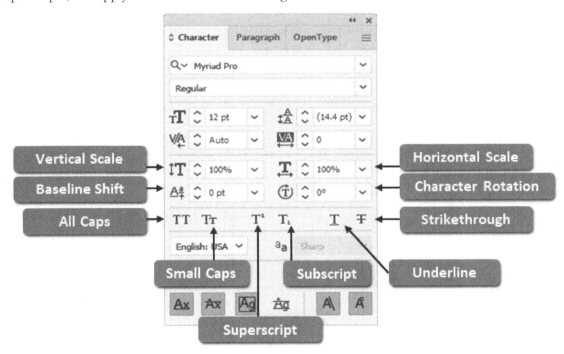

Figure 4-2: The Character panel displaying options to set advanced character formatting settings.

Color Type	Description
Vertical Scale	Increases or decreases the height of a character. You can assign a percentage value that specifies the relative change in height between the original character and the transformed character.
Horizontal Scale	Increases or decreases the width of a character. You can assign a percentage value that specifies the relative change in width between the original character and the transformed character.

Color Type	Description
Baseline Shift	Shifts the baseline of the character so that it is placed above or below the normal baseline.
Character Rotation	Rotates the character by a specified angle.
All Caps	Converts small letters in the selected characters to capital letters.
Small Caps	Converts small letters in the selected characters to capital letters while retaining the letter heights of small letters.
Superscript	Reduces the font size of the selected character and positions it at the top-right corner of the preceding character.
Subscript	Reduces the font size of the selected character and positions it at the bottom-right corner of the preceding character.
Underline	Underlines the selected characters.
Strikethrough	Applies a straight line across the selected characters.

Type to Outlines

In Adobe® Illustrator®, the **Convert Type To Outlines** option gives you endless ways in which to manipulate type. This option allows you to convert any text into outlines so that you can manipulate it into points by using the **Direct Selection** tool. This tool is especially handy when creating logos where you might wish to combine an image with type. To access this tool, select the type object and then select **Type→Create Outlines**.

Figure 4–3: Type to Outlines.

> **Access the Checklist tile on your CHOICE Course screen for reference information and job aids on How to Set Character Formats.**

Do prior to sending to printing co. They might not have your font.

If you send a PDF you will be ok most of the time. Double check proof all looks good.

ACTIVITY 4–1
Setting Character Formats

Data File

C:\092034Data\Formatting Type\Emerald Epicure.ai

Scenario

Your artwork contains most of the drawings needed for the brochure and you have also added text to different pages in your brochure. The second and third pages of the brochure have titles for two of the product descriptions, and the last page has the contact details of Emerald Epicure. You now want to create colorful and attractive titles for the different pages in the brochure and start filling the product descriptions.

1. Open **C:\092034Data\Formatting Type\Emerald Epicure.ai**. If the **Missing Fonts** dialog box appears, select **Close** to accept the font substitution.

2. Add the company's name to the front cover of the brochure.
   a) If necessary, in the **Layers** panel, select the **Text** layer.
   b) In the **Tools** panel, select the **Type** tool. **T.**
   c) On the artboard **1**, above the oil bottle, click the artboard and type *Emerald Epicure*

3. Apply character formats to the company name on the brochure cover.
   a) Select the text **Emerald Epicure**.
   b) Open the **Character** panel.

   If necessary, expand the collapsed dock of panels. If it is not in the docked panels, from the **Menu** bar, select **Window→Type→Character**.
   c) From the **Character** panel menu, select **Show Options**.

   If options are already shown, the menu option is **Hide Options** and you can just close the panel menu.
   d) In the **Set the font family** drop-down list, select **Calibri**.
   e) From the **Set the font style** drop-down list, select **Bold**.

Note: If in the font drop-down list Calibri is followed by an asterisk, then it is not available on your computer. For purposes of this activity, select a font without an asterisk.

f) From the **Set the font size** drop-down list, select **36 pt**.

4. Apply color to the title.

a) Use the **Selection** tool to select the **Emerald Epicure** type object.

b) Drag the type object and position it in such a way that the top-left corner of the bounding box is at approximately **7.2** inches on the horizontal ruler and **1.4** inches on the vertical ruler.

If you are having trouble moving just the text and instead are moving the rectangle and the text, from the **Select** menu, select **Next Object Above** to move just the text.

c) In the **Swatches** panel, scroll down, and locate the **My Pantone Plus Library**.

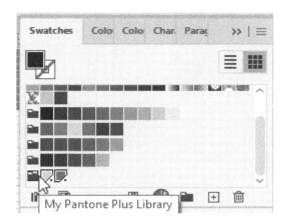

d) Select the first color to apply yellow fill color to the text.

e) Select **Edit→Edit Colors→Convert to CMYK** to convert the **Pantone Plus** color to the **CMYK** color mode.

f) Select in the scratch area to deselect the text.

5. Add text within the rectangle below the oil bottle.

a) In the **Tools** panel, select the **Type** tool.

b) In the **Character** panel, from the **Set the font style** drop-down list, select **Italic**.

c) From the **Set the font size** drop-down list, select **21 pt**.

d) Select in the middle of the rectangle below the oil bottle.

e) Type *Olives and Our Lives*

f) Select the text that you typed.

g) In the **Swatches** panel, select the **My New Swatch** color swatch to apply dark green color to the text.

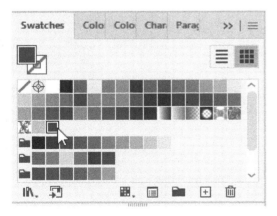

h) Use the **Selection** tool to select the type object and position it at the center of the rectangle.

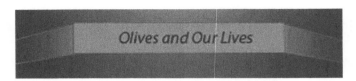

6. Create a title for the product descriptions on the brochure.

a) Select artboard **2** to view the top-left corner of the artboard on the right.

b) In the **Tools** panel, select the **Type** tool.

c) Click above the **Live Paint** group containing the curved path and type *Olives and Our Lives*

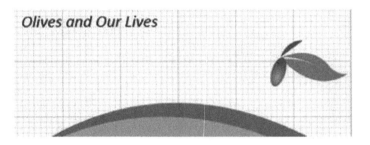

d) Select the text **Olives and Our Lives**.

e) In the **Character** panel, from the **Set the font family** drop-down list, verify that **Calibri** is selected and from the **Set the font style** drop-down list, select **Bold**.

f) From the **Set the font size** drop-down list, select **36 pt**.

g) In the **Swatches** panel, select the fifth color (green) in the second row.

7. Rotate the letter Oin Olives.

a) Use the **Selection** tool to select the **Olives and Our Lives** type object.

b) Drag the type object and position it so that its top-left corner is at approximately **0.1** inches on the horizontal ruler and **0.4** inches on the vertical ruler.

c) In the **Tools** panel, select the **Type** tool.

d) Select the letter O in the word **Olives**.

e) In the **Character** panel, in the **Character Rotation** text box, replace "0°" with *10* and press **Enter**.

f) Observe that the letter "O" is rotated by 10 degrees.

8. Adjust the spacing between characters.

a) Click between the characters O and l in the word **Olives**.

b) In the **Character** panel, from the **Set the kerning between the two characters** drop-down list, select **-25**.

c) Observe that the spacing between the letters "O" and "l" is reduced.

d) Save the file as *C:\092034Data\Formatting Type\My Emerald Epicure.ai*

e) In the **Illustrator Options** dialog box, select **OK** to accept the default settings.

f) Leave the file open for the next activity.

TOPIC B

Apply Advanced Formatting Options to Type

You set character formats for text. The text in your document may not always contain standard characters. Suppose you are creating an invitation for an event and you want to use ornamental characters. By using the advanced formatting options in Illustrator, you can style text to suit your preferences. In this topic, you will apply advanced formatting options to type.

Color and Appearance of Type

The color and appearance of type objects can be changed by applying fills, strokes, transparency settings, effects, and graphic styles. As long as you don't rasterize it, the text can be edited. When you change the color of a type object, Illustrator will overwrite the attributes of the individual characters in that type object. You can use the **Control** panel to quickly change the type's color.

Types of Fonts

You can view samples of how different fonts look by using the font family and font style menus in the **Character** panel, as well as any other area in the application where you can select fonts. Notice to the right of the sample text, different icons are displayed. These icons indicate which type of font you are viewing

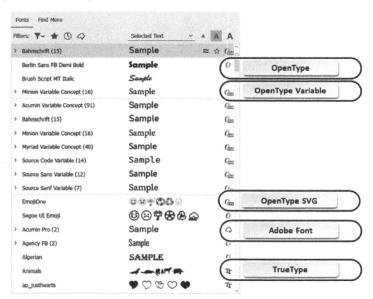

Figure 4-4: Viewing font samples in the Character panel.

OpenType Features

OpenType fonts offer additional features—such as standard ligatures, contextual alternates, swash, stylistic alternates, titling alternates, ordinals, and fractions—which you can apply to characters in type. However, not all OpenType fonts support all these features. By using the options in the **OpenType** panel, you can specify the OpenType features that you want to apply.

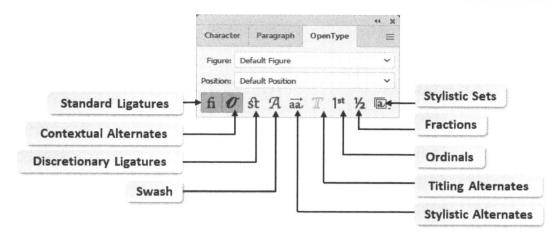

Figure 4-5: Options to set OpenType features in the OpenType panel.

Anti-aliasing

Anti-aliasing is a technique that you can use to smooth jagged edges of type. Setting anti-aliasing options enhances the appearance and readability of text. The four anti-aliasing options you can set to type are **None**, **Sharp**, **Crisp**, and **Strong**. You can set anti-aliasing options to each text frame, and Illustrator saves the values you set as part of your document.

Figure 4-6: Set the Anti-aliasing option in the Character dialog box.

> **Access the Checklist tile on your CHOICE Course screen for reference information and job aids on How to Apply Advanced Formatting Options to Type.**

ACTIVITY 4–2
Applying Advanced Formatting Options to Type

Before You Begin
My Emerald Epicure.ai file is open.

Scenario
Some text in your brochure has been formatted with OpenType fonts. You want to make use of the features supported by these fonts to enhance the appearance of the text.

1. Format the mailing address text in the "CONTACT US" section.

   a) Scroll to the bottom-left corner of artboard 1 to view the address text.

   b) If necessary, on the **Menu** bar, select **Window→Type→Character** to open the **Character** panel.
   c) On the artboard, using the **Type** tool, select the two-line address.
   d) In the **Set the font family** drop-down list, select **Calibri**.

2. Apply the **Standard Ligatures OpenType** to the selected address text.

   a) In the **Tools** panel, verify that the **Type** tool is selected.
   b) In the **Character** panel group, select the **OpenType** tab to display the **OpenType** panel.
   c) From the **Figure** drop-down list, select **Tabular Oldstyle**.
   d) Set the **Zoom** level to **300%** to focus on the selected text.
   e) Observe how the letters "f" and "i" appear in the street name.

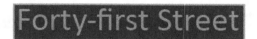

   The first two letters in "first" are combined.

f) In the **OpenType** panel, deselect the **Standard Ligatures** button.

Forty-first Street

Because the change can be subtle, you might want to toggle the **Standard Ligatures** button several times to make sure you've seen the change.

g) Toggle back to enable the **Standard Ligatures**.

3. Apply the **Stylistic Alternates** to the selected text.

a) In the address, select the word **Binghamton**.

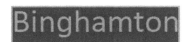

b) Observe the letter "g."

c) In the **OpenType** panel, select the **Stylistic Alternates** button.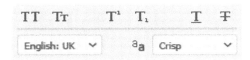

d) Observe that the letter "g" in the word "Binghamton" has changed.

Binghamton

4. Set anti-aliasing options for the document.

a) In the **Tools** panel, select the **Selection** tool to deselect the **Type** tool.

b) Select the **Character** panel.

c) From the **Set the anti-aliasing method** drop-down list, select **Crisp** to set the anti-aliasing method for the document.

TT Tr	T¹ T₁	T F
English: UK ⌄	ᵃₐ	Crisp ⌄

If these options are not displayed, from the **Character** panel menu, select **Show Options**.

d) Close the **Character** panel group.

e) Save and close the file.

Serif vs San serif font
has the tail
or feet

Summary

In this lesson, you formatted type. You can now enhance the appearance and readability of text in your artwork.

Which character or OpenType formatting option would you want to use frequently in your documents? Why?

Which formatting options will you prefer to apply to adjust character spacing and enhance the appearance of the paragraphs in your artwork?

 Note: Check your CHOICE Course screen for opportunities to interact with your classmates, peers, and the larger CHOICE online community about the topics covered in this course or other topics you are interested in. From the Course screen you can also access available resources for a more continuous learning experience.

5 Enhancing the Appearance of Artwork

Lesson Time: 1 hour

Lesson Introduction

Improving the appearance of your artwork will not stop with formatting type in your document. Imagine that you are creating a sales catalog for your company. You have added several photographs and product descriptions to this catalog. However, the sales manager wants the catalog to look unique so that it attracts customers. You can make the objects in the catalog stand out by using various Adobe® Illustrator® features such as effects, blends, masks, symbols, and graphic styles. In this lesson, you will enhance the appearance of artwork.

Lesson Objectives

In this lesson, you will:

- Apply effects to an object.

- Create graphic styles.

- Apply a mask to an object.

- Create symbols and work with symbol sets and symbolism tools.

- Create 3D objects.

TOPIC A

Apply Effects to an Object

You enhanced the appearance of text in your artwork to ensure that it stands out. You may now want to enhance the appearance of other objects in your artwork so that they also grab the attention of the document's audience. In Illustrator, you can enhance objects without changing their structure. In this topic, you will apply effects to an object.

Effects

An *effect* is an appearance attribute that you can apply to an object, a group, or a layer. Once you apply an effect, Illustrator alters the object's appearance without changing its underlying structure. Effects do not alter an object's appearance permanently. The effects added to an object are listed in the **Appearance** panel. By using the options in the **Appearance** panel, you can edit, delete, duplicate, or hide the effects applied to an object.

 Note: You can apply effects to bitmap images and vector graphics. However, you cannot apply an effect to a linked bitmap image. To apply an effect to a bitmap image, you must embed the image within the document.

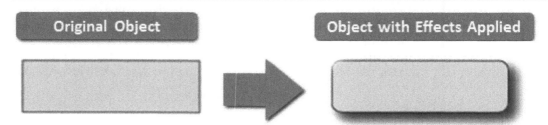

Figure 5-1: Original object and the object with effects applied to it.

 Note: To learn more about applying effects, check out the LearnTO **Apply Effects to Objects** presentation from the **LearnTO** tile on the CHOICE Course screen.

Types of Effects

Illustrator provides two types of effects—*Illustrator effects* and *Photoshop effects*. Some Illustrator effects are vector effects that you can apply only to vector graphics or to the fill or stroke of a vector object. However, other Illustrator effects such as 3D effects, SVG filters, Warp effects, Transform effects, Drop Shadow, Feather, Inner Glow, and Outer Glow are exceptions and can be applied to both vector and bitmap objects.

Photoshop effects are raster effects that you can apply to both vector and bitmap objects. The effects gallery helps you control the appearance of Photoshop effects.

The Illustrator and Photoshop effects are available under various categories.

Illustrator Effects Category	Description
3D and Materials	Makes a 2D object look like a 3D object by applying **Plane**, **Extrude & Bevel**, **Revolve**, or **Rotate** effects, as well as applying various materials to objects and specifying lighting for the selected object.

Illustrator Effects Category	Description
Convert to Shape	Converts an object to a rectangle, a rounded rectangle, or an ellipse.
Crop Marks	Adds crop marks around an object.
Distort & Transform	Reshapes an object by distorting and transforming it.
Path	Applies effects that offset an object's path, converts type to a set of editable paths, or converts the stroke of an object into a filled object.
Pathfinder	Combines objects to create a complex illustration that is editable.
Rasterize	Converts a vector object to a raster object.
Stylize	Styles objects by feathering edges, adding inner and outer glows, and applying drop shadows, rounded corners, or scribbles.
SVG Filters	Applies XML-based graphic effects to an object. Effects include **Bevel Shadow**, **Gaussian Blur**, **Turbulence**, and so on.
Warp	Distorts or deforms objects by using effects such as **Arcs**, **Bulge**, **Squeeze**, and so on.

Photoshop Effects Category	Description
Artistic	Applies an artistic effect, such as colored pencil or watercolor, to simulate artwork.
Blur	Blurs pixels next to the hard edges of an image to smooth the edges.
Brush Strokes	Adds brush strokes to an object to make it look as if it was painted by hand.
Distort	Geometrically distorts and reshapes an object.
Pixelate	Sharpens an object by clustering pixels with similar color values.
Sketch	Makes the object appear like a realistic drawing that is hand-drawn on paper.
Texture	Adds a texture to an object to create an illusion of depth or provide an organic look to it.
Video	Optimizes an object for video.

Raster Effect Options

Raster effect options ensure that the appearance of raster effects remains consistent across all types of media. You can set these options in the **Document Raster Effect Settings** dialog box. The raster effect options you can set are **Color Model**, **Resolution**, **Background**, **Anti-alias**, **Create Clipping Mask**, **Add Around Object**, and **Preserve Spot Colors**.

Options for Commonly Used Effects

The options that you can set for an effect depend on the type of effect you have selected. The options available for some of the commonly used effects are listed in this table.

Effect	Available Options
Drop Shadow	• Mode • Opacity • X Offset • Y Offset • Blur • Color • Darkness • Preview
Inner Glow	• Mode • Color • Opacity • Blur • Center • Edge • Preview
Outer Glow	• Mode • Color • Opacity • Blur • Preview
Feather	• Radius • Preview
Gaussian Blur	• Radius • Preview

Appearance Panel Group

In the **Appearance** panel group, you can adjust attributes for an object, a group, or a layer. Listed in the **Appearance** panel are fills, strokes, effects, and opacity. You can either adjust an already assigned fill, stroke, or opacity, or you can assign a new one. You can also toggle the attribute on or off if you would like to see the new attribute in comparison to the object without it. Effects are displayed in the **Appearance** panel.

The other panel in this panel group is the **Transparency** panel. You can specify a blending mode and the opacity percentage for the selected object. From the panel options menu, you can show a thumbnail of the selected object.

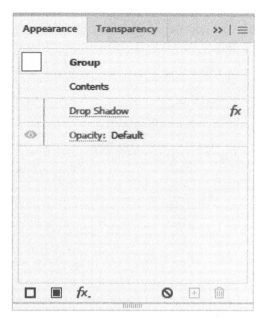
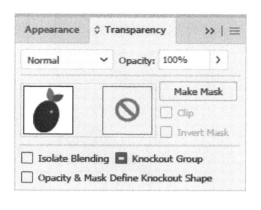

Figure 5-2: The Appearance panel group.

Object Distortion

Although an object can be distorted in many different ways, one of the most common ways to distort an object is to use an envelope. An envelope is an object that is added to a selected object that reshapes or distorts it. You can either create a new envelope or you can use one of the preset warp shapes or preset mesh grids.

To distort an object by using an envelope, select the desired object. Then select **Object→Envelope Distort→Make with warp**. Select the desired warp style or set options in the **Warp Options** dialog box. This option creates a preset warp shape. To create a rectangular grid for the envelope, select **Object→Envelope Distort→Make With Mesh**. You will then configure the desired number of rows and columns in the dialog box.

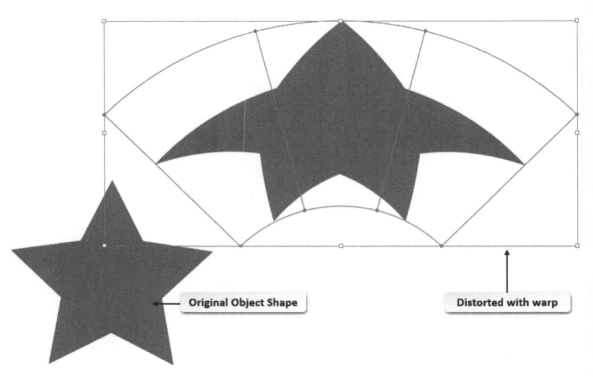

Original Object Shape

Distorted with warp

Figure 5-3: Object distortion with warp.

 Access the Checklist tile on your CHOICE Course screen for reference information and job aids on How to Apply Effects to an Object.

ACTIVITY 5–1
Applying Effects to an Object

Data File

C:\092034Data\Enhancing the Appearance of Artwork\Emerald Epicure.ai

Scenario

You added drawings of olive leaves and fruits to your brochure. You want to enhance the appearance of these drawings by applying different effects to them.

---

1. Open **C:\092034Data\Enhancing the Appearance of Artwork\Emerald Epicure.ai**. If necessary, select **Close** to accept the font substitutions.

2. Add a drop shadow effect to the olives.
    a) Go to the second artboard.
    b) In the graphic below the title "Olives and Our Lives," select the two olives. (You might want to increase the Zoom level to 200%.)

    c) Select **Effect→Stylize→Drop Shadow** to apply the drop shadow Illustrator effect.

     Note: Use the **Stylize** command in the **Illustrator Effects** section.

    d) In the **Drop Shadow** dialog box, in the **Mode** drop-down list, verify that **Multiply** is selected.
    e) Set the **X Offset** to *-0.01*
    f) Set the **Y Offset** to *0*
    g) Set the **Blur** to *0.03* and select OK.
    h) Observe that a drop shadow is applied to the olives.

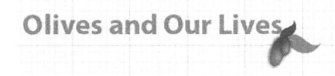

3. Apply a drop shadow effect to the other olives in the brochure.

---

a) On artboard **1** view the olives with leaves above and to the right of the text "Skin Care Oil" on the left artboard.

b) Select the two olives.
c) Select **Effect→Stylize→Drop Shadow** to apply the drop shadow Illustrator effect.
d) In the **Drop Shadow** dialog box, select **OK** to apply a drop shadow by using the same settings you applied to the olives in the right artboard.

e) Click in the scratch area to deselect the olives.

4. Create an oil drop.

a) In the **Layers** panel, select the **Text** layer and create a new layer above the **Text** layer.
b) Double-click **Layer 7** and type *Drop* to change the layer name.
c) Verify that the stroke color is set to none.
d) In the **Tools** panel, select the **Fill** button, and in the **Gradient** panel, from the **Type** drop-down list, verify that **Radial** is selected.
e) In the **Gradient Slider**, apply **Black** color to the right gradient stop and **White** color to the left gradient stop.
f) Set the value in the **Angle** text box to **0°**.
g) Set the **Aspect Ratio** to **100%**.

h) Create a circle with a diameter of *0.3* inches and position it at the intersection of **9** inches on the horizontal ruler and **2.5** inches on the vertical ruler so that it appears above the oil bottle.

i) In the **Transparency** panel, from the **Blending Mode** drop-down list, select **Darken**. Change **Opacity** to **30%**.

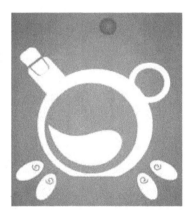

5. Apply a **Gaussian Blur** effect to the oil drop.

a) In the **Drop** layer, create another circle with a diameter of **0.05** inches. Set the fill color of the circle to white and the stroke color to none.

b) Position this white circle within the circle you created earlier in such a way that the white circle is close to the top-left corner of the enclosing circle. (You might want to increase the **Zoom** level to 1200%. Alternatively, you could use the **Transform** to set the X value to about 8.9 and the Y value to about 2.45.)

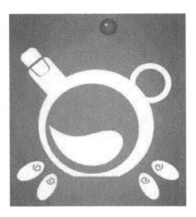

c) Select **Effect→Blur→Gaussian Blur**.
d) In the **Gaussian Blur** dialog box, set the **Radius** to *3*
e) Select **OK** to apply the **Gaussian Blur** effect to the white circle.

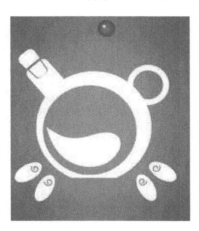

f) Choose **File→Save As**.
g) Navigate to the **C:\092034Data\Enhancing the Appearance of Artwork** folder and save the file as *My Emerald Epicure.ai*
h) In the **Illustrator Options** dialog box, select **OK** to accept the default settings.

6. Create a formatted line.

a) Scroll to the bottom-left corner of the left artboard to view the "CONTACT US" section of the brochure. Make sure the text does not become selected.
b) In the **Layers** panel, select **Layer 1**.
c) In the **Tools** panel, select the **Stroke** button.
d) In the **Swatches** panel, select the fifth color (dark green) in the second row.
e) In the **Stroke** panel, from the **Weight** drop-down list, select **3 pt**.
f) In the **Tools** panel, select the **Line Segment** tool.

g) Above the image of the jar, position the mouse pointer at the intersection of **0.1** inches on the horizontal ruler and **4.3** inches on the vertical ruler and draw a vertical line until it touches the patterned bottom border.

Reminder: If you hold down **Shift** while dragging to create the line, the line will be straight no matter if you move the pointer left or right.

7. Create another straight line at the right end of the page.

a) Deselect the line.

b) In the **Tools** panel, select the **Stroke** button and in the **Swatches** panel, select the first color (light green) in the second row.

c) Create another vertical line at the intersection of **5.9** inches on the horizontal ruler and **4.3** inches on the vertical ruler to the patterned bottom border.

8. Create a blend between the two lines.

a) Select the two vertical lines.

b) In the **Tools** panel, double-click the **Blend** tool.

c) In the **Blend Options** dialog box, from the **Spacing** drop-down list, select **Specified Steps**.

d) In the text box to the right of the **Spacing** drop-down list, replace "8" with *40* and select OK.

e) Use the **Blend** tool to select the top endpoint of the vertical line at the left.

 f) Select the top endpoint of the vertical line at the right.

 g) Observe that a set of vertical lines is created between the two lines, with colors transitioning from dark green to light green.

 h) In the **Tools** panel, select the **Selection** tool to deselect the **Blend** tool.

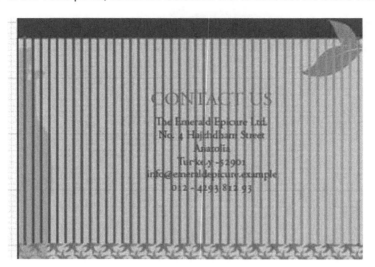

 i) Save the file and leave it open for the next activity.

TOPIC B

Create Graphic Styles

You applied effects to an object. When you use similar objects in a document you may need to apply the same effects and other appearance attributes to each object. This could become a tedious task and may result in errors if you miss applying an attribute to some objects. You can accomplish this easily if you group all those attributes and apply the attributes in a single step. In this topic, you will create graphic styles and apply them to objects.

Graphic Creation

Adobe Illustrator offers many different ways to fill an object, including graphic styles. In some cases you may have applied attributes to a specific object and now wish to apply those attributes to another object. For instance, if an object has a specific gradient applied to it and a specific stroke, you can make it into a graphic style. To do so, go to **Window→Graphic Styles** to display the **Graphic Styles** panel. In the **Graphic Styles** panel, choose the **New Graphic Style** button and assign a name to the new graphic style. After that, when an item is selected, you can click the graphic style to apply it to that item. In the **Graphic Styles** panel, you can create styles, edit styles, and import styles from other documents.

Graphic Styles Libraries

A *graphic styles library* is a collection of preset graphic styles. You can move graphic styles from a graphic styles library to the **Graphic Styles** panel. Though graphic styles libraries open in panels named after them, you cannot add, edit, or delete the graphic styles available in them. However, you can create a new graphic styles library and add graphic styles to it.

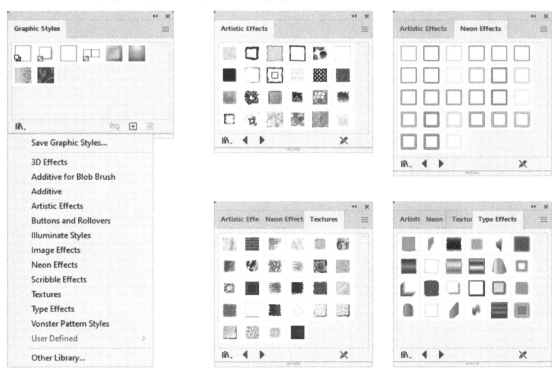

Figure 5–4: Examples of graphic style libraries.

Viewing Attributes for Targeted Objects

In some cases, you may want to change some attributes without affecting others. The targeting column in the **Layers** panel can help you identify objects for which attributes have been set. The targeting column can also help in selecting a given object. The targeting column appears on the right side of the **Layers** panel, next to the layer name and icon. A single circle in the targeting column indicates that the object is not 'targeted' (selected). A double circle indicates the object is targeted. A circle without fill color indicates the object has no attributes beyond fill and stroke color. A circle with fill color indicates the object has attributes beyond fill and stroke color. To change an item's specific attribute, target it by selecting the desired icons in the **Layers** panel. The **Attributes** panel will display the attributes for the object targeted in the **Layers** panel.

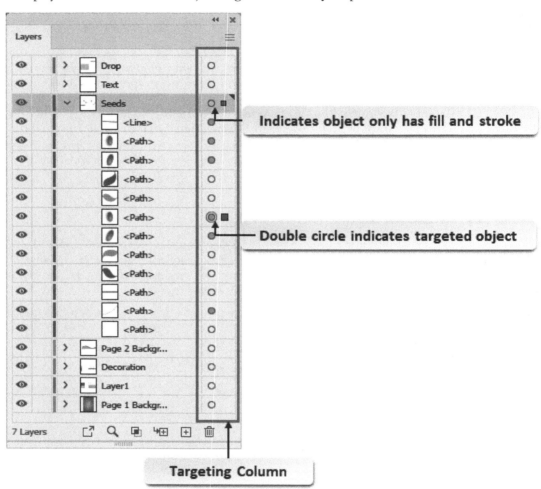

Figure 5–5: Current attributes in the Layers panel.

Access the Checklist tile on your CHOICE Course screen for reference information and job aids on How to Create Graphic Styles.

ACTIVITY 5-2
Creating a Graphic Style

Before You Begin
My Emerald Epicure.ai file is open.

Scenario
You want to underline the title of your brochure. To do this you want to draw a line and enhance its appearance by applying different colors and effects. Instead of selecting new colors and applying effects on this line, you want to reuse the styles you already applied to the olives in your brochure.

---

1. Create a graphic style.

   a) Select the big olive to the right of the text "Skin Care Oil."

   b) Display the **Graphic Styles** panel.
   c) In the **Graphic Styles** panel, select the **New Graphic Style** button.
   d) Observe that the colors and effects applied to the olive are saved as a graphic style.

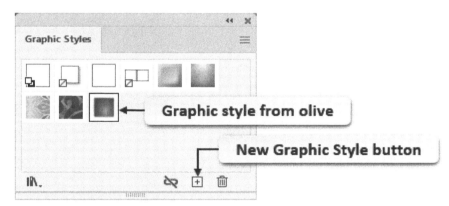

   e) Double-click the new graphic style.
   f) In the **Graphic Style Options** dialog box, in the **Style Name** text box, replace "Graphic Style" with *My Graphic Style* and select **OK**.

2. Create an underline for the title of the brochure.

   a) In the **Tools** panel, select the **Line Segment** tool.

---

b) Draw a horizontal line below the text "Emerald Epicure."

c) In the **Stroke** panel, from the **Weight** drop-down list, select **3 pt**.

d) In the **Graphic Styles** panel, select **My Graphic Style** to fill the line with the graphic style you created.

e) In the **Tools** panel, select the **Stroke** button and select the **Gradient** button below the **Stroke** button to apply gradients in the graphic style to the stroke.

f) Deselect the line and save the file.

3. Leave the file open for the next activity.

TOPIC C

Apply a Mask to an Object

You created a blend to smoothly transition shapes and colors. When you use vector shapes or bitmap images in artwork, you will frequently come across the need to hide portions of an image. By using masks, you can not only hide portions of an underlying object but also control transparency to partially hide the underlying object. In this topic, you will apply a mask to an object.

Masks

A mask is a partially transparent object that shows portions of an image directly below its transparent areas and hides the image below its opaque areas. You can edit a mask and reposition it to show or hide different portions of the masked image.

Figure 5–6: Masks.

There are two types of masks available.

Type of Mask	Description
Opacity mask	An object that shows portions of an underlying image based on varying degrees of transparency of the object. You can vary the degree of transparency by controlling the color of the mask.
Clipping mask	An object or set of objects called a clipping set that hides artwork. Only those portions of the image that are immediately below and within the outline of the clipping mask are visible.

 Note: To learn more about applying masks, check out the LearnTO **Apply Masks** presentation from the **LearnTO** tile on the CHOICE Course screen.

Clipping Masks

A *clipping mask* allows you to use a top shape to create a mask of the artwork that is underneath. To create a clipping mask, create the object or shape that you want to use as the mask, called the clipping path. This can only be a vector object. Move this clipping path and the object that you wish to mask into its own layer or group. The masking object must be at the top of the group or layer in order to work effectively. Then in the **Layers** panel, select the **Make/Release Clipping Masks** button. You can edit the clipping mask from the **Layers** panel, or from the application menu. To release a clipping mask, select **Object→Clipping Mask→Release**.

Figure 5-7: An image masked to display only the portion within a circular clipping mask.

The Knockout Technique

Knockout is a technique that is used to prevent an underlying object from being visible even if objects above it are transparent. It is commonly used to ensure that a dark underlying color does not affect a light overlapping color when printed. In Illustrator, you can prevent an underlying object from being visible through a transparent object or mask by using the knockout technique.

Transparency Knockout Group

An opacity mask, the masked artwork, and the group of objects on which you need to apply the knockout effect comprise a transparency knockout group. In a transparency knockout group, objects lying below other transparent objects in the group are not seen. Only underlying objects that are not in the group are visible.

The Opacity & Mask Define Knockout Shape Option

The **Opacity & Mask Define Knockout Shape** option is used to define the knockout effect applied to a shape. When this option is selected, the knockout effect is proportional to the transparency of the object. If the object is opaque, the knockout will be strong, and if the object is completely transparent, there will be no knockout. If an opacity mask is used with a gradient applied to it, the underlying object will be knocked out depending on the opacity in different areas of the mask.

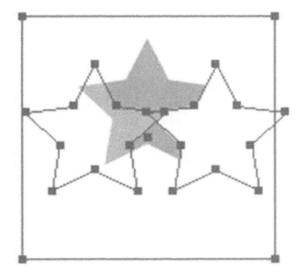

Figure 5-8: Knockout techniques.

 Access the Checklist tile on your CHOICE Course screen for reference information and job aids on How to Apply a Mask to an Object.

ACTIVITY 5-3
Applying Masks to an Object

Data Files

C:\092034Data\Enhancing the Appearance of Artwork\Extra Virgin.png

C:\092034Data\Enhancing the Appearance of Artwork\Light Olive.png

Before You Begin

My Emerald Epicure.ai file is open.

Scenario

You added all the product descriptions to the brochure with relevant titles. You now want to add images for each product. Instead of displaying the images in their default rectangular shapes, you want to present the images in a circular shape. You also want to seamlessly blend them with the background.

---

1. Place an image on the right artboard.

   a) In the **Layers** panel, create a new layer above the **Drop** layer and rename it as *Images*
   b) Show artboard **2** and select **Fit On Screen**.
   c) Select **File→Place**.
   d) In the **Place** dialog box, navigate to the **C:\092034Data\Enhancing the Appearance of Artwork** folder and select **Extra Virgin.png**.
   e) Select **Place** to load the image on the cursor.
   f) Select on the artboard to position it to the left of the text "Extra Virgin Olive Oil" so that it is between the left border of the artboard and the text.

   Move or reposition the image if needed.

2. Create a clipping mask for the image.

   a) Create a circle with a diameter of **2** inches. Fill and stroke the circle with white color.

---

b) Use the **Selection** tool to move the circle and place it on top of the image.

c) Hold **Shift** and select the image.
d) Select **Object→Clipping Mask→Make**.
e) Observe that the circle creates a clipping mask to show portions of the image within the circle and to hide the rest of the image.

3. Apply a 5 point white color stroke to the circle.

a) Double-click the image to create the layer **Isolation Mode**.

b) In the **Layers** panel, observe the single layer "Isolation Mode." Expand both Isolation Mode and Clip Group.

c) Select the **Click to Target** circle for the Ellipse.

d) Observe the double circle in the targeting column.

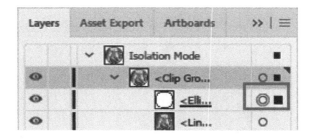

e) Verify a white color stroke was applied to the ellipse.
f) In the **Control** panel, from the **Stroke Weight** drop-down list, select **5 pt** to apply a border to the image.

g) Double-click anywhere on the artboard to exit the **Isolation Mode**.

4. Add an image for the Light Olive Oil product.

   a) Select **File→Place**.
   b) In the **Place** dialog box, navigate to the **C:\092034Data\Enhancing the Appearance of Artwork** folder and select **Light Olive.png** and select **Place**.
   c) Select on the artboard to position the image to the left of the text "Light Virgin Olive Oil."
   d) Create a circle with a diameter of **2** inches. Fill and stroke the circle with white color and place it over the image.
   e) Select the circle and image.

f) Select **Object→Clipping Mask→Make**.

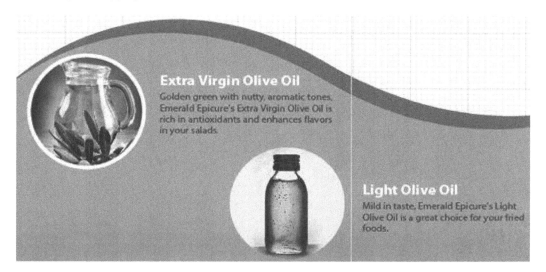

g) Double-click the image to enter the layer **Isolation Mode**.
h) In the **Layers** panel, select the **Click to Target** circle for the ellipse, apply a white color stroke to it, and set the stroke width to **5 pt**.

i) Double-click the artboard anywhere to exit the **Isolation Mode**.

5. Create a rectangle for the opacity mask.
   a) Scroll to the bottom-left corner of artboard **1**.
   b) In the **Layers** panel, create a new layer and rename it as *Contact Us Background*

c) Drag the **Contact Us Background** layer and place it below **Layer 1**.

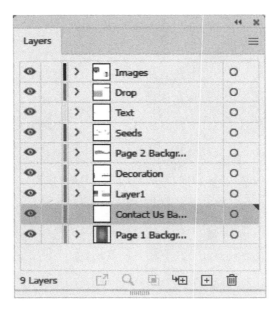

d) In the **Tools** panel, select the **Fill** button, and in the **Gradient** panel, from the **Type** drop-down list, select **Linear**.

e) Apply the **black** color to the gradient stop on the right and **white** color to the gradient stop on the left.

f) In the **Angle** text box, replace "0°" with *90*

g) Draw a rectangle with a width of **6** inches and a height of **3.7** inches. Place it over the "CONTACT US" section so that it covers the light green background entirely.

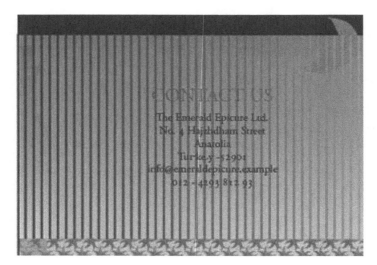

6. Create an opacity mask for the blend of vertical lines.

   a) In the **Layers** panel, expand **Layer 1**. Hold **Shift** and use the **Click to Target** circle to select the **Blend** sublayer.

b) Expand the **Contact Us Background** layer and observe that in the **Layers** panel, both the rectangle you created in the previous step and the blend sublayer display a double circle in the targeting column.

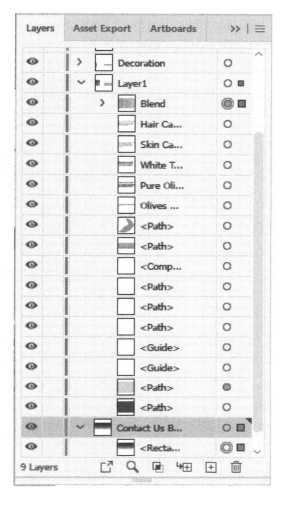

c) In the **Transparency** panel, from the panel menu, select **Make Opacity Mask** to create an opacity mask.

d) Observe that the top portion of the vertical lines is more visible than the bottom portion of the lines.

e) Save the file and leave it open for the next activity.

TOPIC D

Apply Symbols and Symbol Sets

You may have painstakingly created a beautiful vector graphic by using effects, blends, or masks. Imagine the time and effort you have to spend if you need to create multiple copies of this graphic in your artwork. Instead of redoing the graphic repeatedly, you can use symbols to quickly replicate your work.

Suppose you need to alter the appearance of a large number of symbol instances. Imagine the time and effort you would require to ensure a consistent output. By creating symbol sets, you can alter the appearance of multiple symbol instances quickly and consistently. In this topic, you will create symbols and work with symbol sets and symbolism tools.

Symbols

A *symbol* is a reusable art object that serves as a template for creating identical graphics quickly. You can create multiple instances of a symbol and use those instances in your document. You can edit individual symbol instances and customize them without affecting the original symbol. The **Symbols** panel provides access to preset symbols and options for creating new symbols and managing them.

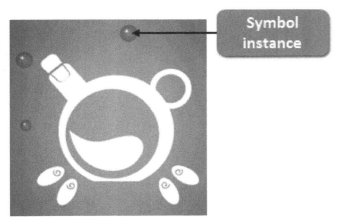

Figure 5-9: Multiple instances of a symbol placed on an artboard.

Symbol Registration Point

The *symbol registration point* is a point in a symbol that is treated as its origin. It is identified by a visible mark that appears when you create or edit the symbol.

Symbol Libraries

A *symbol library* is a collection of preset symbols of a specific type. The symbols in a symbol library appear in a panel named after the library. You can move the symbols in a symbol library to the **Symbols** panel, or add new symbols to a symbol library.

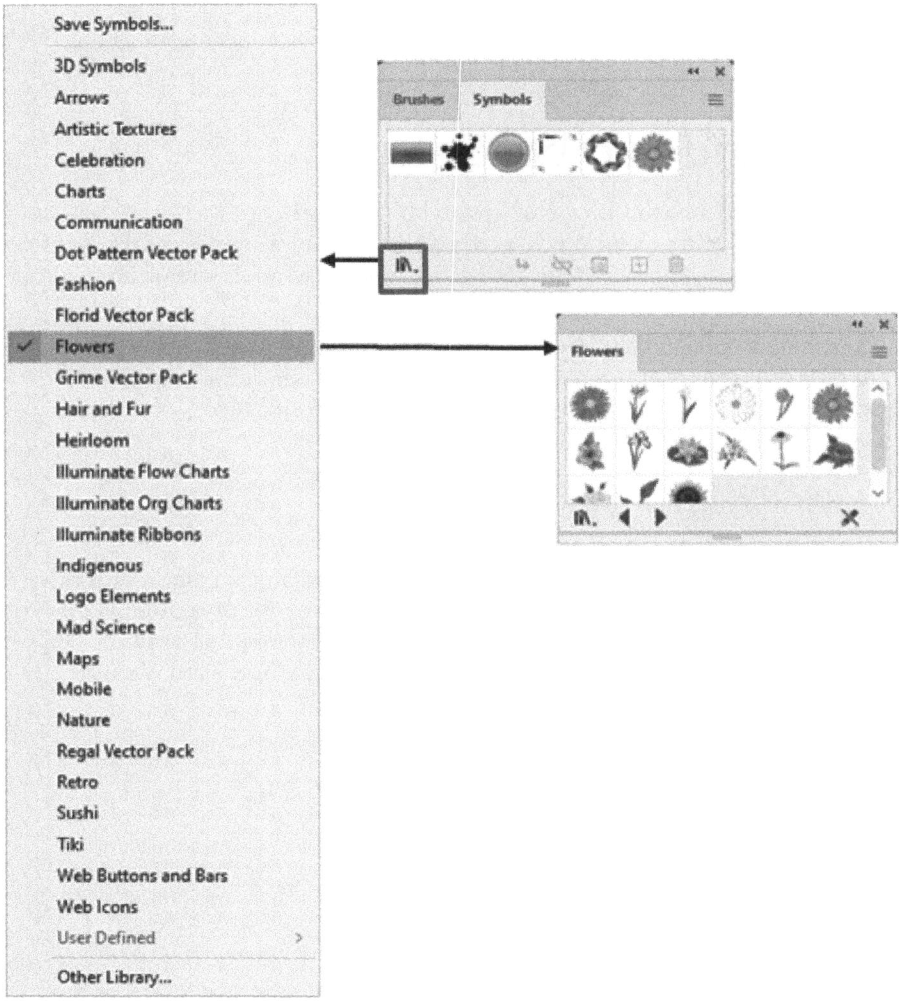

Figure 5-10: The Flowers panel displaying symbols from the Flowers symbol library.

9-Slice Scaling

9-slice scaling is a technique that breaks a symbol into nine imaginary slices and scales each slice independently. The nine slices are displayed as a scaling grid that is visible only in the **Isolation** mode. The grid appears as dotted lines over the symbol. The scaling grid displays grid lines at 25 percent of its width and height from all four sides of the symbol's bounding box. When the symbol is scaled, the slices along the edge are scaled relatively lesser than the center slice. By using 9-slice scaling, you can scale vector and bitmap symbols while maintaining the visual integrity of the symbol.

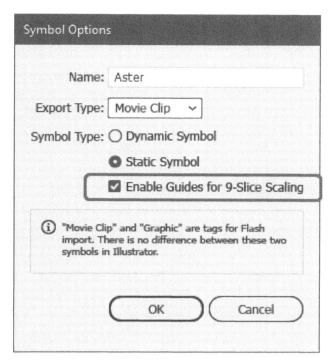

Figure 5-11: 9-slice scaling.

Symbol Sets

A *symbol set* is a group of symbol instances. By using symbol sets, you can mix different types of symbol instances and create complex artwork.

Figure 5-12: Symbol instances in a symbol set.

Symbolism tools help you create symbol sets and modify the size, appearance, density, color, transparency, and style of symbol instances in a symbol set. These tools help you add sets of identical objects to artwork and modify them easily.

Symbolism Tool	Description
Symbol Sprayer	Creates a symbol set by spraying instances of the selected symbol on the artboard.
Symbol Shifter	Moves symbol instances in a symbol set in one direction and changes their stacking order.
Symbol Scruncher	Gathers or scatters symbol instances in a symbol set across the artboard.
Symbol Sizer	Resizes symbol instances in a symbol set and alters their density.
Symbol Spinner	Alters the orientation of symbol instances in a symbol set.
Symbol Stainer	Changes the hue of the symbol instances without altering the luminosity of the original color.
Symbol Screener	Increases or decreases the transparency of symbol instances.
Symbol Styler	Applies to or removes graphic styles from symbol instances. You can control the degree to which the selected graphic style is applied to the symbol instances.

Symbolism Tool Options

The symbolism tool options help you control the way symbol instances are created and modified. You can set these options by using the **Symbol Tool Options** dialog box.

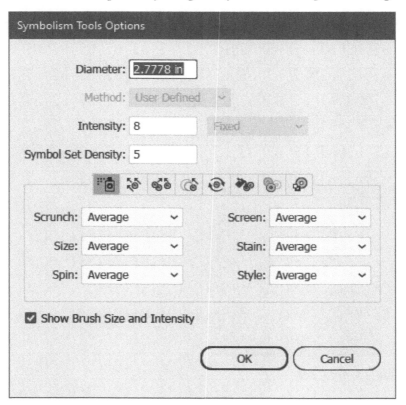

Figure 5-13: Symbolism Tool options.

Symbolism Tool Option	Description
General Options	Specify settings for the diameter of the brush, symbol set density and intensity, and the method used to modify symbol instances. These options are common to all the symbolism tools.
Symbol Sprayer Options	Control the way symbol instances are created by specifying values for the **Scrunch**, **Size**, **Spin**, **Screen**, **Stain**, and **Style** attributes. You can either select the average values of existing symbol instances, or specify user-defined values. **Note:** These options appear only when the **Symbol Sprayer** tool is selected.
Symbol Sizer Options	Control whether symbol instances are resized uniformly and specify whether resizing symbol instances affects their density. These options appear only when the **Symbol Sizer** tool is selected.

Graphs and Charts

A graph is a great way to communicate information that includes statistics. In Adobe Illustrator, you can create a graph that conveys this information by using the **Graph** tool. Once the **Graph** tool is selected, drag to create a box in which you want to hold the graph. You can also draw the graph from its center by holding **Alt** while dragging. You will then enter the data that you want to include in the graph into the **Graph Data** window.

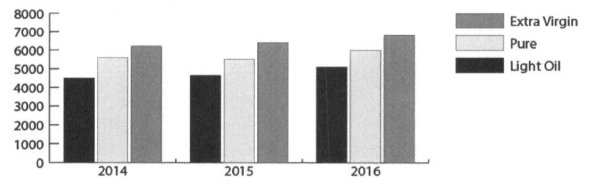

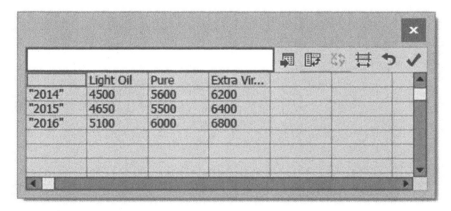

Figure 5-14: Graphs and charts.

Symbols and Representative Graphics

To create a more impactful graph or chart, you can add symbols and other representative graphics. This could include joins, logos, or other symbols that might represent a specific value. The options for graph designs include a vertically scaled design, uniformly scaled design, repeating design, and a sliding design. In all of these designs, a specific symbol or graphic is used to represent an amount or an item. These symbols graphics are then manipulated to convey the information depending on which kind of graph design you choose.

Figure 5–15: Symbols and representative graphics.

 Access the Checklist tile on your CHOICE Course screen for reference information and job aids on How to Apply Symbols and Symbol Sets.

ACTIVITY 5-4
Applying Symbols and Symbol Sets

Before You Begin

My Emerald Epicure.ai file is open.

Scenario

You want to add oil droplets at different locations on the front cover of the artboard to make the front cover more appealing. You created an oil drop earlier and you want to reuse it to create multiple instances. You want to fill the background of the front cover of your brochure with oil drops of different sizes. You want to apply oil drops of different sizes while maintaining consistent appearance and style.

1. Create a symbol out of the oil drop.
   a) On the front cover, just above the oil bottle, select the oil drop.
   b) Hold **Shift** and select the small circle within the oil drop.
   c) Right-click and select **Group** to group the two objects.

   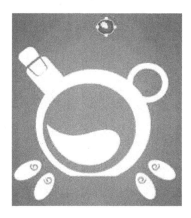

   d) Select the **Symbols** panel.
   e) Select the **New Symbol** button to create a symbol out of the oil drop.

    Note: When you create a new symbol, by default, the selected artwork becomes a symbol instance for the new symbol. To prevent the selected artwork from becoming a symbol instance, hold **Shift** when you select the **New Symbol** button.

   f) In the **Symbol Options** dialog box, in the **Name** text box, type *Oil Drop*

g) In the **Symbols** panel, observe that the new symbol is added in the second row.

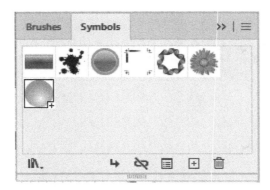

2. Create multiple instances of the **Oil Drop** symbol.

   a) In the **Symbols** panel, verify that the **Oil Drop** symbol is selected.

   b) In the **Symbols** panel, select the **Place Symbol Instance** button. ⤷

   c) Observe that an instance of the **Oil Drop** symbol is added on the artboard.

   d) Drag the symbol instance and position it close to the oil bottle's cap.

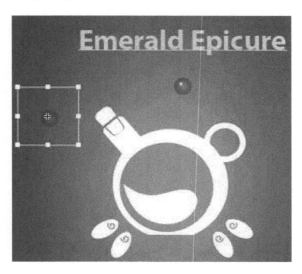

   e) In the **Symbols** panel, select the **Place Symbol Instance** button to create another instance.

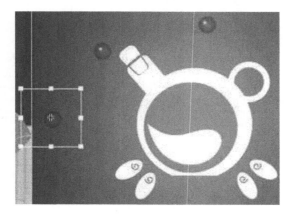

f) Drag the resizing handles to reduce the size of the instance and move it an inch closer to the oil bottle.

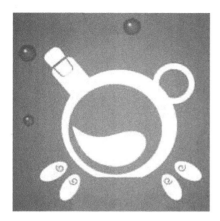

g) Click anywhere on the artboard to deselect the symbol instance.
h) Save the file.

3. Set symbolism tool options.

a) In the **Tools** panel, double-click the **Symbol Sprayer** tool.
b) In the **Symbolism Tools Options** dialog box, set the **Diameter** to *2*
c) Set the **Symbol Set Density** to *3*
d) From the set of symbolism tools below the **Symbol Set Density** text box, select the **Symbol Sizer** tool.
e) Uncheck the **Resizing Affects Density** check box and select **OK**.

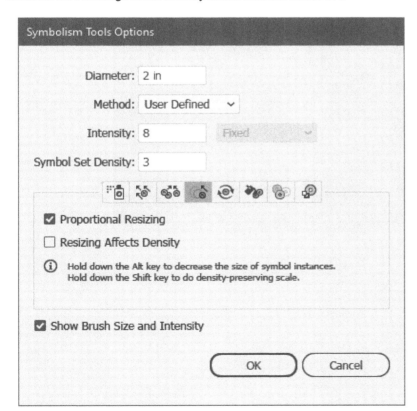

4. Create a symbol set.

   a) In the **Symbols** panel, verify that the **Oil Drop** symbol is selected.

   b) In the **Tools** panel, from the **Symbol Sizer** tool menu, select the **Symbol Sprayer** tool.

   c) Click the artboard at approximately **6.9** inches on the horizontal ruler and **5.5** inches on the vertical ruler to create the first symbol instance of the symbol set.

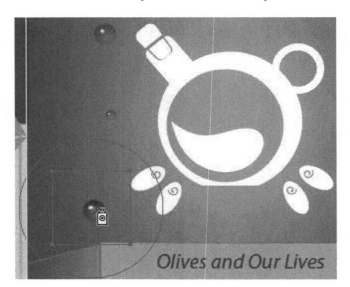

   d) Click the artboard at approximately **11** inches on the horizontal ruler and **5** inches on the vertical ruler to create another symbol instance.

   e) Observe that a rectangle enclosing the two symbol instances appears.

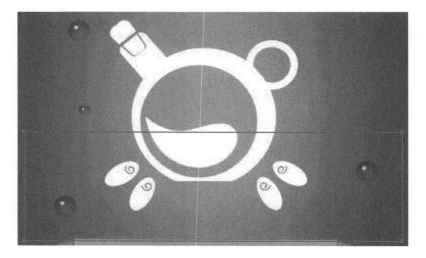

f) Create a third symbol instance at approximately **10.7** inches on the horizontal ruler and **5.4** inches on the vertical ruler.

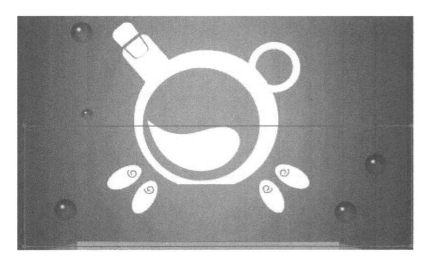

5. Modify symbol instances in the symbol set.

a) In the **Tools** panel, from the **Symbol Sprayer** tool menu, select the **Symbol Sizer** tool.

b) Hold **Alt** and click twice on the first symbol instance to reduce its size.

c) Hold **Alt** and click three times on the third symbol instance to reduce its size.

d) In the **Tools** panel, from the **Symbol Sprayer** tool menu, select the **Symbol Shifter** tool.

e) Drag the second symbol instance you created to approximately **10.8** inches on the horizontal ruler and **3.9** inches on the vertical ruler.

f) Observe that the symbol instance has moved to the desired location.

g) Save and close the file.

TOPIC E

Work with 3D Objects

So far, you have been working in two-dimensional artworks, even when you apply perspective to the objects. Illustrator allows you to make objects appear to be 3D by adjusting the shading and other properties of an object.

3D Effects

The **Effects** menu provides several ways you can create 3D objects from 2D vector graphics. You can also select the 3D effect to apply from the **3D and Materials** panel. A simple ellipse can become a tube, a plumbing joint, a ball, and more. In the following figure, all of the objects started out as copies of the original 2D object. The 3D effect can also be applied to text.

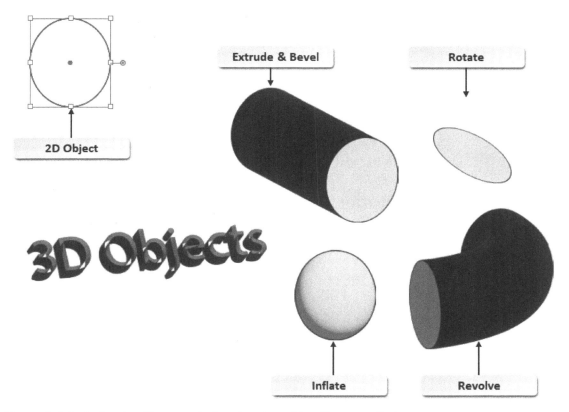

Figure 5–16: A simple ellipse copied and various 3D effects applied.

3D and Materials Panel

When you select a 3D effect to apply to an object, the **3D and Materials** panel opens so you can configure the 3D effect on the selected object. The available options in the panel are based on which 3D type is selected.

You can create symmetrical 3D objects with Bevel and Inflate 3D effects. If you select the **Inflate both sides** option, this will create a symmetrical 3D object.

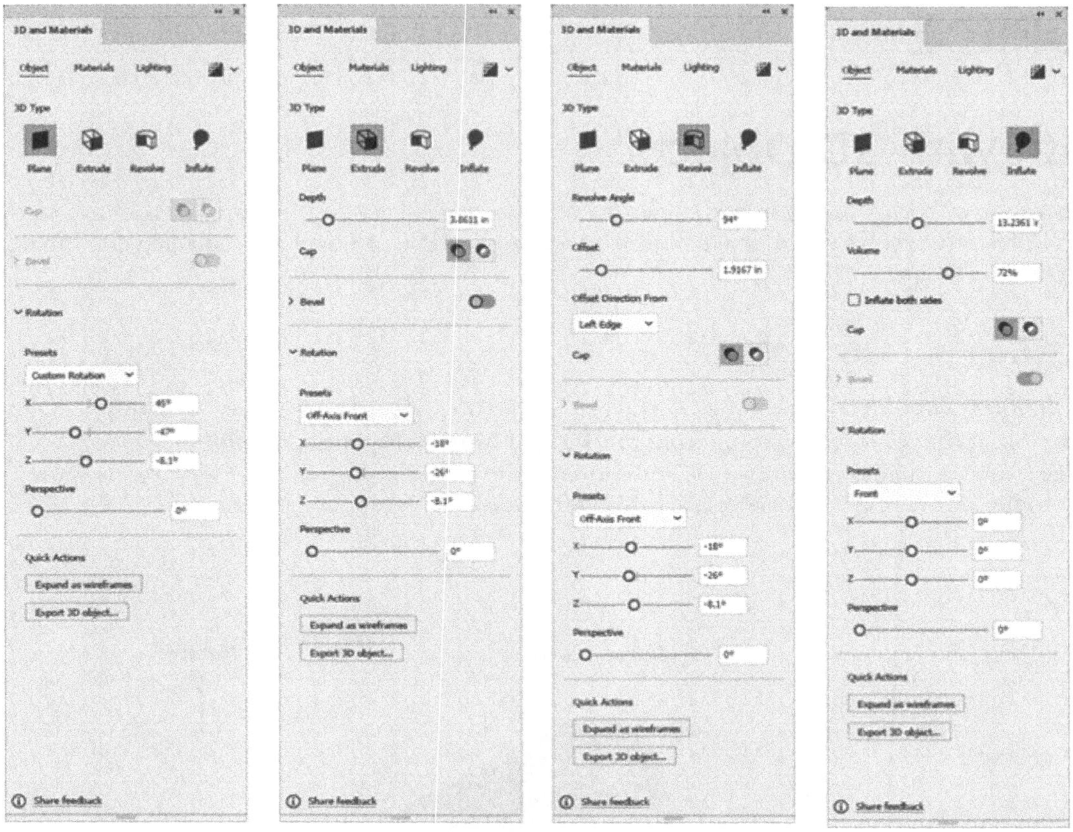

Figure 5-17: The 3D and Materials panel Object panel for each 3D Type.

Adobe Substance Materials

The **Materials** tab of the **3D and Materials** panel provides access to the various materials and graphics that can be applied to a 3D object. In addition to the **Adobe Substance Materials** available by default, you can download additional substance materials from Substance 3D assets or from the Substance 3D Community assets.

Figure 5-18: 3D objects with various Adobe Substance Materials applied.

Artwork Map

3D objects contain multiple surfaces and you can map 2D artwork to each of those surfaces. 2D artwork stored in the **Symbols** library can be mapped to 3D objects. The symbols can include Illustrator artwork, paths, text, raster images, mesh objects and more.

You can select **Invisible Geometry** to suppress the 3D object's display so that only the mapped artwork is displayed. This effect can give the illusion of movement of the text or object to which the artwork was mapped.

3D Object with Vector Graphic

You can render map artwork as a vector graphic along with a 3D object. Adding an image as a graphic in the **3D and Materials** panel allows you to apply the graphic to a 3D object.

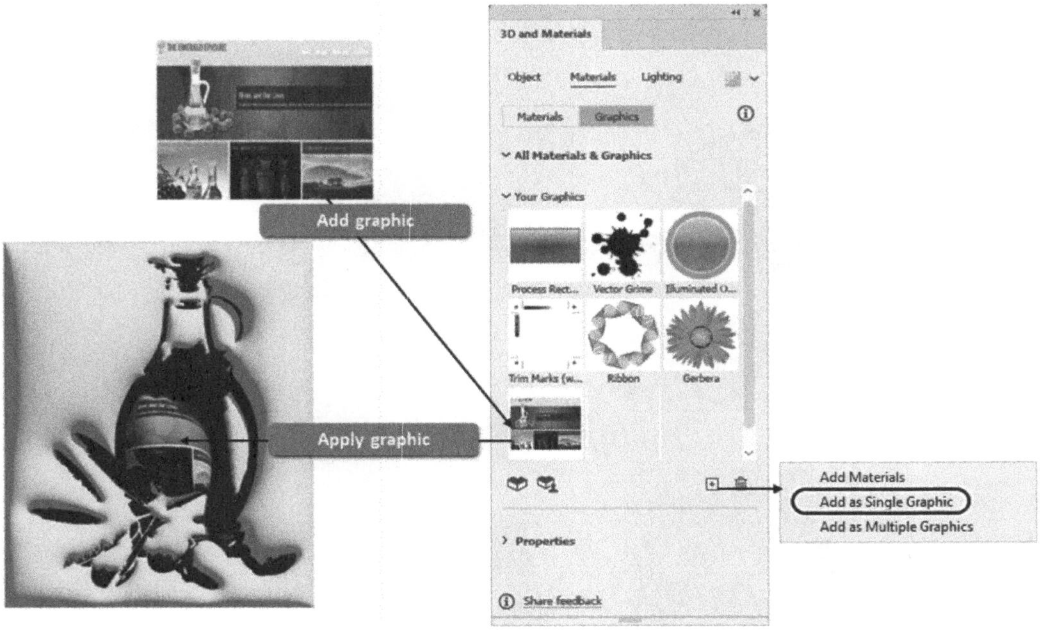

Figure 5-19: A graphic saved to 3D Materials and applied to a 3D object.

3D Object Perspective

When you create a 3D extruded and beveled object or a revolve object, the **Position** setting determines how the object looks from the viewer's point of view. In addition to the preset positions, you can change the angle in the **Perspective** text box.

To get the effect of viewing the object through a telephoto lens, use a smaller angle. To get the effect of viewing the object through a wide-angle lens, use a larger angle. If the angle extends past the viewer's point of view, the object will appear distorted.

You can also adjust the perspective on the X, Y, and Z axes, where X is horizontal, Y is vertical, and Z is perpendicular in relation to the viewer.

Rectangle with 3D effects:
- Extruded
- Bevel Inside
- Perspective: 0°

Rectangle with 3D effects:
- Extruded
- Bevel Inside
- Perspective: 90°

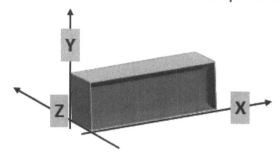

Figure 5-20: Two perspectives with the X, Y, and Z axes identified.

Wireframes

You can use a wireframe to outline the contour of an object. This makes each surface of the 3D object transparent. If you create a wireframe, it is a good idea to do it on a copy of the original image, so you don't lose the original image.

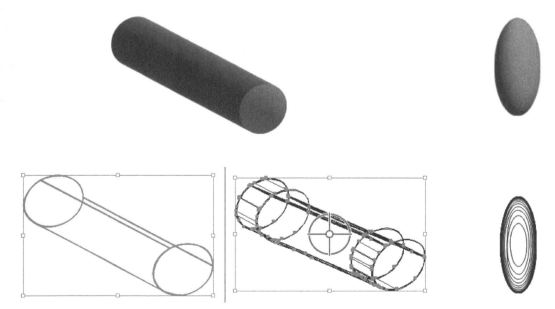

Figure 5-21: Original objects and their related wireframes.

Shadow Alignment

The **Lighting** tab of the **3D and Materials** panel includes a **Shadows** section. If you enable shadows, you can then select the position of the light source, the distance from the object, and the bounds of the shadow. The preset positions allow you to quickly and easily align the shadow with the 3D object.

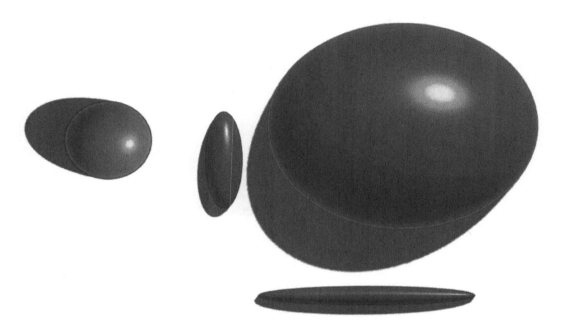

Figure 5-22: Examples of how shadows align with objects.

Wireframes for Shading

Wireframes can be useful when shading an object because they show the underlying structure of a 3D object. This allows you to be accurate in where the light would hit the object in the real world.

3D Object Export

One of the **Quick Actions** in the **3D and Materials** panel is the **Export 3D object** button. This opens the **Asset Export** panel. 3D assets can be exported in several formats including PNG, USDA, or OBJ file formats. If you export 3D objects as OBJ files, the objects are exported along with colors defined for the 3D object. You can export to multiple file formats at the same time. You can also select the scaling factor for the file and can export multiple scaling factors to export at the same time.

For export objects that are intended for mobile devices, preset options for iOS® and Android™ output can be selected. These generate the file output types typically used for each of those operating systems.

Exported 3D objects can be imported into the **Adobe Substance 3D Stager** or other applications that support 3D objects.

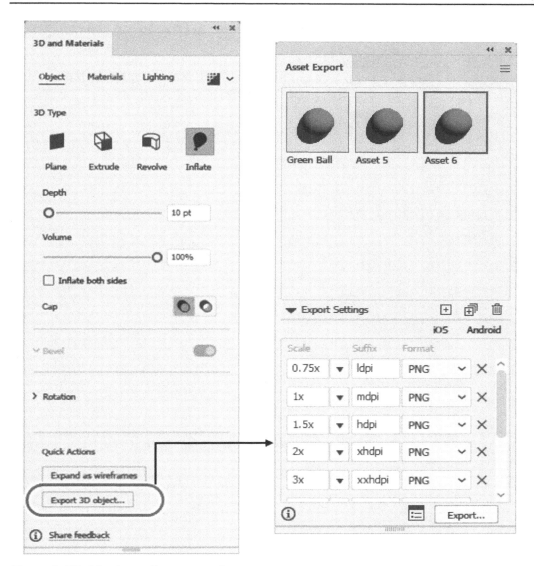

Figure 5-23: The Asset Export panel.

Render with Ray Tracing

The **Render with Ray Tracing** button on the **3D and Materials** panel is useful after you apply the desired 3D effects to your objects. This feature helps you in creating more realistic 3D effects by showing you how the light would bounce over the object, and tracing the path of the light rays. The quality of the 3D image is affected by the **Document Raster Effect Settings** resolution setting. The **Render as vector** option will not be applied if your artwork uses materials or graphics with gradients or raster images. It can take some time for complex 3D images to render.

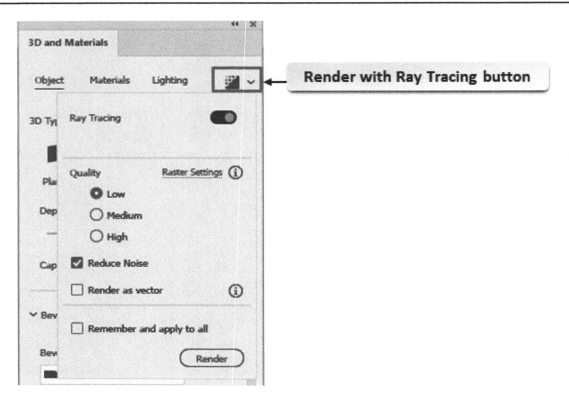

Figure 5-24: The Render with Ray Tracing options.

Access the Checklist tile on your CHOICE Course screen for reference information and job aids on How to Work with 3D Objects.

ACTIVITY 5–5
Working with 3D Objects

Data File

C:\092034Data\Enhancing the Appearance of Artwork\3D Examples.ai

Scenario

You recently attended a meeting where the presenter had used 3D images and you noticed how impactful the images were. A colleague has some examples they used recently and shared the file with you. You want to take a look at those images and then try your hand at creating some 3D images.

---

1. Open **C:\092034Data\Enhancing the Appearance of Artwork\3D Examples.ai**.

2. Examine the rectangular object on artboard 1.
   a) With artboard **1** selected, set the zoom level to **Fit On Screen**.
   b) Select **Window→3D and Materials**.
   c) On the artboard, select the blue and gray box at the top of the artboard.
   d) In the **3D and Materials** panel, examine the **3D Type** for the box.
      This rectangle has the **Extrude** type applied.

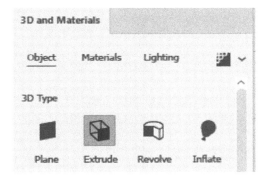

No longer in Photoshop

e) Examine the **Bevel** settings for the box.

The **Bevel** setting has been enabled and the **Bevel Shape** is set to **Round**. The **Bevel Inside** and **Bevel both sides** are checked to give the appearance that the original blue square has become an inset in a box shape.

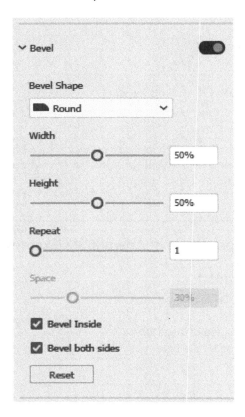

3. Examine the elliptical shapes on artboard 1.

a) Select the tubular shape on artboard **1**.

This is also an extruded 3D type, but a shadow has been added to the object.

b) In the **3D and Materials** panel, select the **Lighting** tab, then scroll down to view the settings in the **Shadows** section.

The **Shadows** option is enabled and the **Position** is **Below Object** at a distance of 9%.

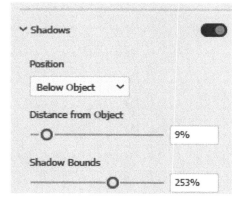

c) Select the round elliptical object and observe that the shadow settings are directly behind the object at 0% distance.

d) Select the elongated elliptical object and observe that no shadow settings have been applied.

4. Apply graphics to an object.

    a) Select the round elliptical object on artboard 1.

    b) In the **3D and Materials** panel, select the **Materials** tab.

    c) Expand **Your Graphics**, then select **Gerbera Daisy**.

    d) Resize the graphic to roughly the same size as the round ball.

    e) In the **3D and Materials** panel, in the **Properties** section, check **Invisible Geometry**.

    f) Observe the image and the shadow.

       The green ball is no longer shown and the shadow is a shadow of the petals on the daisy.

    g) Uncheck **Invisible Geometry**.

       The ball is back and the shadow is of the ball rather than the daisy petals.

5. Apply 3D **Rotation** and **Perspective** settings to a **Plane** 3D type object.

    a) Switch to artboard 2.

    b) Select and copy the green rectangle, then paste it on artboard 2.

    c) With the copied rectangle selected, in the **3D and Materials** panel, in the **3D Type** section, select **Plane**.

       The object is slightly rotated using the values in the **Rotation** section **Presets** of **Off-Axis Front**.

    d) Experiment with various **Presets** and **Perspective**.

6. Apply Extrude settings to an object.

    a) Paste another copy of the rectangle below the original rectangle.

    b) Change the **Stroke** to a contrasting color such as red.

       This will help make the changes you set more obvious as you adjust settings.

    c) In the **3D and Materials** panel, on the **Object** tab, select **Extrude**.

    d) Experiment with changing the **Depth** and the **Cap** on the object.

    e) Enable **Bevel**, the adjust the **Bevel Shape**, **Width**, **Height**, **Repeat**, and **Space** as desired.

7. Apply **Revolve** settings to an object.

    a) Paste a copy of the rectangle on artboard 2.

    b) Copy and paste a copy of the circle on artboard 2.

    c) Select both copied objects, then in the **3D and Materials** panel, select **Revolve**.

    d) Compare the results of the two objects.

       Even though the rectangle started out with 90 degree angled corners, it is now a cylinder. The circle looks like a tire or donut.

    e) Experiment with changing the **Rotation** and **Perspective** on each of the objects.

8. Apply **Inflate** settings to an object.

    a) Paste copies of the rectangle and circle on artboard **2**.

    b) With the rectangle selected, select **Effect→3D and Materials→Inflate**.

       You can change the settings from the menu as well as in the panel.

    c) Experiment with various **Depth**, **Volume**, and **Rotation** values.

    d) With the circle selected, select **Inflate**.

    e) With the circle selected, select **Effect→3D and Materials→Inflate**.

    f) Experiment with various **Depth**, **Volume**, and **Rotation** values.

9. Add shadows to objects.

    a) Select any object on artboard **2**.

    b) In the **3D and Materials** panel, select the **Lighting** tab.

    c) Set the **Shadows** slider to enable shadows.

    d) Experiment with the **Position** and **Distance from Object** settings to see how it changes the shadow.

    e) Apply shadows to another object if desired.

10. Save changes and close the file.

    a) Save the file as *My 3D examples*

    b) Close the file.

Summary

In this lesson, you enhanced the appearance of artwork by using different techniques. Although effects enhance the visual appeal of an object, masks and blends enable you to control the display of objects with ease. You also used 3D effects to increase the realistic look to objects.

Imagine that you are creating a pamphlet for a company that promotes organic food. You want to create aesthetic designs to make your pamphlet look attractive. What effects will you most likely apply to the objects in your pamphlet to achieve this?

Give examples of when you will choose to create symbols in Illustrator.

Note: Check your CHOICE Course screen for opportunities to interact with your classmates, peers, and the larger CHOICE online community about the topics covered in this course or other topics you are interested in. From the Course screen you can also access available resources for a more continuous learning experience.

6 Preparing Content for Deployment

Lesson Time: 1 hour, 30 minutes

Lesson Introduction

You applied different types of effects to your artwork. Having enhanced your artwork with different techniques, you would want to ensure that it appears as expected when printed. Printers use different technologies and settings to reproduce artwork. To ensure that your artwork prints identically and exactly the way you want it, you need to prepare it for printing. In this lesson, you will prepare content for deployment.

Lesson Objectives

In this lesson, you will:

- Set up artwork for printing.

- Prepare transparent artwork and manage colors for printing.

- Create slices and image maps.

- Save artwork in the SVG format and save graphics for the web.

- Prepare documents for video.

- Prepare files for other applications.

TOPIC A

Prepare Artwork for Printing

You applied effects to objects in your artwork to take your artwork to completion. You are now ready to output the artwork. When artwork is sent for commercial printing, it may not be reproduced exactly as you see it on your monitor. So, before printing your artwork, you may need to ensure that all the colors and effects you applied to objects print correctly. In this topic, you will set up artwork for printing.

Print Dialog Box Options

The options in the **Print** dialog box enable you to specify different settings for printing your document. The **Print** dialog box organizes these options into seven categories. The default settings for these options depend on the startup profile you selected while creating the document.

Category	Options
General	Selects artboards to be printed, orientation of media, print preset to be used, layers to be printed, and document scaling.
Marks and Bleed	Specifies settings for output of the printer's marks and bleeds.
Output	Sets the output mode and printer resolution.
Graphics	Specifies printing fonts and options for printing paths, gradients, and meshes.
Color Management	Determines the way a printer handles colors in a document and specifies the rendering intent for printing.
Advanced	Specifies settings for overprints and transparency flattening.
Summary	Lists a summary of the options selected in the other categories.

Document Scaling

Document scaling options in the **Print** dialog box enable you to scale a document's height and width so that it can be printed on the selected media. For example, if you want to print the artwork on a sheet of paper that is smaller than the size of the artwork, you can scale the artwork to a size that can be fit on the paper.

Figure 6–1: The Print dialog box displaying options in the General category.

Composites

A *composite* is a printed proof of the artwork as it appears on the screen. It helps verify whether all the colors in the document print correctly. Composites also help verify image resolution and identify errors that may occur during commercial printing.

Print Presets

A *print preset* is a collection of settings that automatically specifies values for the options in the **Print** dialog box. You can create your own print preset by specifying all the options you need for printing and save them as a print preset. Print presets save and load print settings, enabling you to automate print jobs for different types of printers.

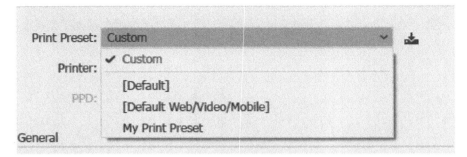

Figure 6-2: Print presets.

Printer's Marks and Bleeds

Printer's marks are marks that a printer needs to precisely align components of an artwork. A document can have four types of printer's marks—trim marks, registration marks, color bars, and page information. A bleed is the amount of space by which the artwork is extended outside the printing area. It serves to minimize trimming errors. You can specify the extent of bleed in your artwork to ensure that Illustrator prints portions of artwork outside the trim marks.

Figure 6-3: Printer's marks and bleeds.

Maximum Blend Length for Gradients

The number of changes in colors in a gradient is the number of steps in the gradient. This number is based on the percentage of change among gradient colors and determines the maximum length of the gradient or blend after which banding occurs. You can determine the maximum blend length for gradients by multiplying the number of grays the printer can print with the percentage change in color.

Printer Resolution and Screen Frequency

Printer resolution is the number of dots that the printer prints per inch of paper. Laser printers commonly have a printer resolution of 600 dots per inch (dpi) while the most common inkjet printers have a printer resolution between 300 and 720 dpi.

Screen frequency is the number of lines or rows of *halftone* dots per linear inch on a screen. A high value for screen frequency displays images by using a large number of dots to create a fine rendering of the image. A low value for screen frequency displays images by using a small number of dots to create a coarse rendering of the image. For the best printing results, you must select a printer resolution that matches the selected screen frequency.

Package Files

Once an Adobe® Illustrator® file is finished and ready for printing, a **Package File** is a great way to organize the attached linked graphics, fonts, and the document and the package report. This ensures that everything about the file is ready for handoff. The included report provides information about all the files. To package an Illustrator file, select **File→Package**. In the **Package** dialog box, specify the location and settings. In the specified location, a folder structure will be created that includes a folder for fonts, a folder for links, the package report, and the Illustrator file.

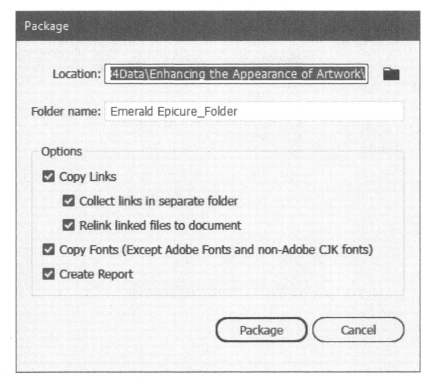

Figure 6-4: Package Files.

Share for Review

If you want other people to review your Illustrator document prior to sending it for printing, you can use the **Share for review** feature. This feature does not require the other people to have Adobe IDs or Illustrator subscriptions. After creating a link to the document and sending or posting the link where others can access it, the link can be used to open the document and provide feedback. You can set the level of access for others. If you change the settings and create a new review link, comments can only be added through the most recent review link

Permission	Access
Only invited people can comment	Requires an email be sent to the person that contains a link to the document to be reviewed.
Anyone with the link can comment	This is a public link that provides everyone with access to the document to be reviewed. Sending an email invitation to people is optional.
Everyone at your organization can comment	Everyone within the owner's email domain can access the document to be reviewed. The document needs to be saved in Creative Cloud for everyone to access the document. No link is required to be sent.

Shared Comments

Using the link or the shared documents list, access the document to review it. You can add comments and draw on the artboards. A message is sent to the document owner when comments have been added. The person making the comment can go back into the comment and edit the content if needed. The owner or the commenter can delete the comment.

Figure 6-5: A document with comments.

 Access the Checklist tile on your CHOICE Course screen for reference information and job aids on How to Prepare Artwork for Printing.

ACTIVITY 6–1
Preparing Artwork for Printing

Data File

C:\092034Data\Preparing Content for Deployment\Emerald Epicure.ai

Scenario

You have completed the brochure by adding all the images for your products and giving it the finishing touches. Before handing off the brochure for commercial printing, you want to make sure that the artwork will print correctly.

---

1. Open **C:\092034Data\Preparing Content for Deployment\Emerald Epicure.ai.** If necessary, select **Close** to accept the font substitutions for the missing fonts.

2. Select the printer and printing layout.
   a) Select **File→Print**.
   b) In the **Print** dialog box, in the **Print Preset** drop-down list, verify that **[Default]** is selected.
   c) From the **Printer** drop-down list, select the **Adobe PDF** printer.
      If Adobe PDF is not available on your computer, select **Microsoft XPS Document Writer**.
   d) In the **Orientation** section, verify that the **Auto Rotate** check box is checked.
   e) From the **Print Layers** drop-down list, select **All Layers**.

3. Specify options for printer's marks and bleed marks.
   a) In the left pane, select the **Marks and Bleed** category.
   b) In the **Marks and Bleed** section, check the **Trim Marks** check box.
   c) From the **Trim Mark Weight** drop-down list, select **0.125 pt**.
   d) Check the **Page Information** check box to display information, such as the artboard number and date and time of printing, in the printed document.
   e) In the **Offset** text box, enter *0.1*
   f) In the **Bleeds** section, verify that the **Use Document Bleed Settings** check box is checked.

4. Specify options for rasterizing gradients and meshes.
   a) In the left pane, select the **Graphics** category.
   b) In the right pane, check the **Compatible Gradient and Gradient Mesh Printing** check box.
   c) In the **Adobe Illustrator** message box that warns you to use this option only when you have problems with gradients and meshes, select OK.

5. Save the settings as a print preset.
   a) To the right of the **Print Preset** drop-down list, select the **Save** button.
   b) In the **Save Print Preset** dialog box, in the **Save Preset As** text box, type *My Print Preset* and select OK.
   c) In the **Print** dialog box, select **Print**.
   d) In the **Save PDF File As** dialog box, browse to **C:\092034Data\Preparing Content for Deployment**.
   e) In the **File name** text box, enter *My Printed Emerald Epicure*

---

f) In the **Save as type** drop-down list, verify **PDF files (*.PDF)** is selected.

g) Select **Save**.

h) Examine the PDF file in Adobe Acrobat looking at print quality, marks and bleed settings, and page information. When finished, close the file.

i) In Illustrator, select **File→Save As**.

j) Navigate to the **C:\092034Data\Preparing Content for Deployment** folder and save the file as *My Print Emerald Epicure.ai*

k) In the **Illustrator Options** dialog box, select **OK**.

l) Leave **My Print Emerald Epicure.ai** open for the next activity.

TOPIC B

Prepare Transparency and Colors for Printing

You prepared your document for printing to avoid errors when the document is printed. In addition to gradients, meshes, and color blends, transparency is another component of artwork that may appear differently when your artwork is saved in different output formats. For example, you may introduce transparency to view an underlying object that is predominantly white. But if the artwork is printed on media of a color other than white, the entire artwork will look different. To ensure that transparent artwork prints as expected, you need to set transparency flattening options.

You set up artwork for printing so that possible issues due to transparency are overcome. Your document should now print as expected. But unfortunately, not all printers can print documents uniformly as they appear on screen. Each printer may have a different color space and color management system. To make sure that all the colors in your document print correctly, irrespective of the printer used, you need to set the document up for printing.

In this topic, you will prepare transparent artwork for printing and manage the colors in your document for printing.

Flattening

Flattening is a process that Illustrator performs to prepare transparent artwork for printing. Illustrator also applies flattening when you save or export your artwork to file formats that do not support transparency. Flattening isolates transparent areas that overlap other objects. It rasterizes the isolated areas and leaves the rest of the artwork as vectors.

You can specify flattening settings and save them as transparency flattener presets so that Illustrator can flatten other transparent objects using the same settings.

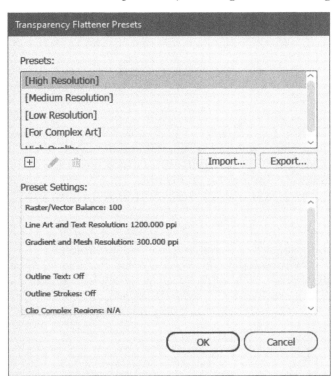

Figure 6-6: Configuration of Transparency Flattener Presets.

> **Note:** You cannot undo flattening once you apply it and save the file.

File Formats that Retain Transparency

File formats such as AI9 and later, AI9 EPS and later, and PDF 1.4 and later support transparency. Artwork saved in these file formats retains transparency.

Print Multiple Artboards

Often times an Illustrator file includes several different artboards. Illustrator offers a way to print those multiple boards on one page or as individual pages. You can print all of the artboards, or you can choose to print a range of artboards. In the **Print** dialog box, select **All** to print all artboards. Select **Range** to specify specific artboards. Or, to print everything on a single page, select **Ignore Artboards**.

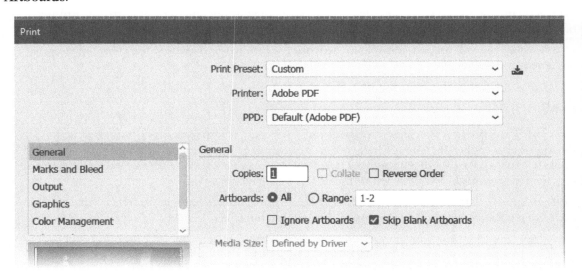

Figure 6–7: Multiple artboards.

Rasterize Artwork

Adobe Illustrator is a vector artwork program. What this means is that all of the artwork you create will be in vector format. If you experience difficulty printing a gradient or a mesh, convert it to a raster image. To do so, select **File→Print**. On the left column of the **Print** dialog box, select **Graphics**, then select **Compatible Gradient and Gradient Mesh Printing**.

Color Separation

Color separation is the process by which a document's contents are separated into four plates. Each plate contains portions of the artwork corresponding to one process color. In addition, if the artwork contains spot colors, then a separate plate for each spot color in the artwork is created. When printing the document, the print technician inks each plate with the respective colors, registers them with one another, and prints them so that the colors combine to reproduce the artwork.

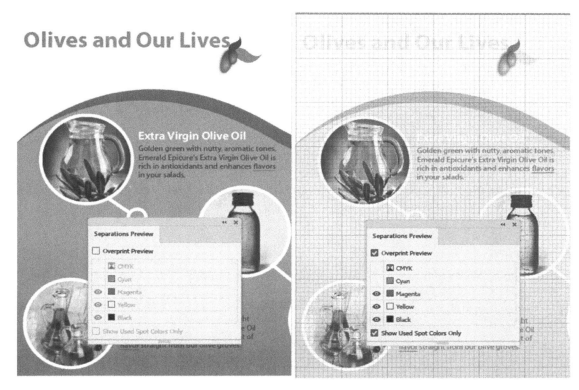

Figure 6–8: Comparison of full colors and color separation preview of a document.

Prepare Artwork for Color Separation

Before printing color separations, it is a good idea to preview the color separations in your document. If your document's color mode is RGB, you must convert it to CMYK. To ensure that your artwork prints smoothly, optimize color blends, set up overprinting and trapping, and preview areas affected by transparency flattening before printing color separations.

Printing Gradients, Meshes, and Color Blends

In some cases, an Illustrator document that includes gradients, meshes, or color blends will not print smoothly. To ensure that it does, use blends that change at least 50 percent between the other process components. You can also use shorter blends and lighter colors. If possible, use a printer that supports PostScript language level 3.

Overprinting

Overprinting is a printing technique that is used to prevent knockouts. When printing artwork that contains overlapping colors, by default, the top-most color prints and knocks out the colors beneath it. A **knockout** is a part of an image that has been removed by an image overlapped on top of it. The bottom color is "knocked out"; that is, not printed, where the other color overlaps. Ordinarily, you would not want the overlapping colors to be printed. If you printed both the top and bottom color, you would potentially have a portion of the image over-saturated with ink. The overlap could also affect the color of the image.

In some cases, you may want both the top and bottom colors to print, but with the top color allowing the bottom color to show through. By using overprinting, you can ensure that the topmost color does not prevent the underlying color from printing; instead, it appears transparent. The choice of ink, paper, and printing method determine the degree of transparency in overprinting.

Overprinting Black Settings

The **Overprint Black** option in the **Print** dialog box overprints black color in your artwork. You can set up overprinting to be applied for objects that are filled with a specific percentage of black. Overprinting with black helps prevent gaps in your artwork.

Trapping

Trapping is a printing technique that helps close gaps among adjoining colors by creating a small area of overlap. While printing artwork using different plates, a mistake in the registration of the plates can result in gaps among overlapping colors.

You can use two types of traps—spread and choke—to close these gaps. A spread is a trap in which a lighter object overlaps a darker background. A choke is a trap in which a lighter background overlaps a darker object.

Trap Options

You can use the **Trap** command to create traps. By using the options of the **Trap** command, you can specify settings for the trap that you need to create.

Illustrator Effect	Description
Thickness	Specifies the extent of the trap. You can set a value between 0.01 and 5,000 points.
Height/Width	Sets the ratio of the trap along the horizontal and vertical directions. You can specify this ratio by using percentage values. By default, the setting is 100 percent, indicating that horizontal traps and vertical traps are equal.
Tint Reduction	Reduces the tint of lighter colors that are trapped.
Traps With Process Color	Converts traps that contain spot colors into process color traps.
Reverse Traps	Reverses darker color traps into lighter color traps.
Precision	Determines the preciseness of the trap. Higher values for precision result in more accurate trapping.
Remove Redundant Points	Removes repeating points from the trap.

 Access the Checklist tile on your CHOICE Course screen for reference information and job aids on How to Prepare Transparency and Colors for Printing.

ACTIVITY 6-2
Preparing Transparency and Colors for Printing

Before You Begin

My Print Emerald Epicure.ai file is open.

Scenario

You have several transparent areas in your artwork because you created masks and changed the opacity of objects. Now, you want to ensure that these transparent areas print properly. You also want to preview the individual color separations. Then you will save the document in the proper format to hand off for printing.

---

1. Create a transparency flattener preset.

   a) Select **Edit→Transparency Flattener Presets**.

   b) In the **Transparency Flattener Presets** dialog box, in the list of presets, select **[High Resolution]**.

   c) Select the **New** button.

   d) In the **Transparency Flattener Preset Options (New)** dialog box, in the **Name** text box, replace "[High Resolution] copy" with *High Quality*

   e) From the **Line Art and Text Resolution** drop-down list, select **1600** and select **OK**.

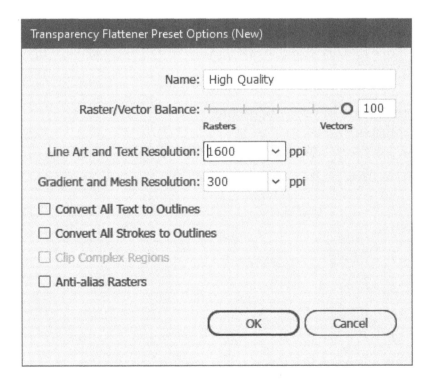

   f) In the **Transparency Flattener Presets** dialog box, in the list of presets, verify that the **High Quality** preset you created is selected and select **OK**.

2. Set transparency flattening options for the document.

a) Select **File→Print**.
b) In the **Print** dialog box, in the **General** category, in the **Printer** drop-down box, verify that **Adobe PDF** is selected.
c) In the left pane, scroll down and select the **Advanced** category.
d) In the right pane, in the **Overprint and Transparency Flattener Options** section, from the **Preset** drop-down list, verify **High Quality** is selected.
e) Select **Done**.

3. Preview transparency flattening.

a) Select **Window→Flattener Preview**.
b) In the **Flattener Preview** panel, select **Refresh**.
c) From the **Highlight** drop-down list, select **Transparent Objects**.
d) Observe that in the preview area, all transparent portions of your artwork are highlighted.

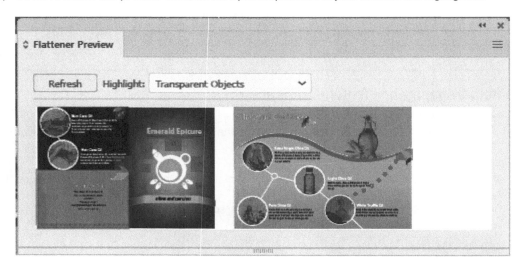

e) Close the **Flattener Preview** panel.
f) Save the file.

4. Preview color separations in your document.

a) Select **Window→Separations Preview**.
b) In the **Separations Preview** panel, check the **Overprint Preview** check box.
c) In the list of inks, in the **Yellow** ink row, select the **Eye** icon 👁 to hide the yellow separation ink.

d) Observe the changes in the document.

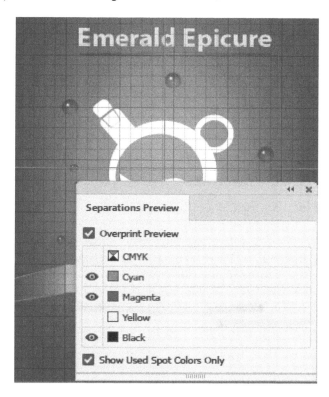

e) Select the **Eye** icon section in the **Yellow** ink row again to show the yellow separation ink.

f) Uncheck the **Overprint Preview** check box to return to normal view.

g) Close the **Separations Preview** panel.

5. Set up the document for color separation.

a) Select **File→Print**.

b) In the **Printer** drop-down list, verify that **Adobe PDF** is selected.

c) In the left pane, select **Output** category.

d) In the right pane, from the **Mode** drop-down list, select **Separations (Host-Based)**.

e) Check the **Overprint Black** check box to enable overprinting of black ink.

6. Verify the **Color Management** settings.

a) In the left pane, select the **Color Management** category.

b) In the **Color Handling** drop-down list, verify that the **Let Illustrator determine colors** option is selected and select **Done**.

c) Save the file.

7. Save the document as a PDF file.

a) Select **File→Save As**.

b) In the **Save As** dialog box, from the **Save as type** drop-down list, select **Adobe PDF (*.PDF)** and select **Save**.

c) In the **Save Adobe PDF** dialog box, select the **View PDF after Saving** check box and select **Save PDF**.

d) Observe that the contents of the brochure you created are displayed in a PDF file.

e) Close the **Adobe Reader** window.

f) In Illustrator, close the **My Print Emerald Epicure.pdf** file.

TOPIC C

Create Slices and Image Maps

Apart from using your artwork in printed material, you will often use it on the web as well. As a graphic designer developing images suited for websites, you need to balance image size and quality. Slices and image maps enable you to optimize images for web display. In this topic, you will create slices and image maps.

Best Practices for Creating Web Graphics

It is important to ensure that images used on websites are optimized to download quickly and display clearly. Some of the best practices for creating web graphics are:

- Balancing image quality with file size: Create images with moderate size so that they are more suitable for graphic distribution on the Internet. Web servers hosting the website can store and transmit images in an efficient manner and viewers can quickly download images. You can use the **Save For Web** dialog box to optimize the image size and download time for a web graphic.
- Choosing the best file format for your graphic: Save graphics in file formats, such as JPEG and PNG, which are better suited for display in websites.

Slices

Slices are smaller rectangular areas of a large web image. Large images are sliced to smaller ones so that each small slice is of optimal size. Slices allow different portions of a large image to be saved in different formats with different settings. For example, in a large web bitmap image, you can use a slice to isolate a complex area of the image and save that slice in the JPEG format, while simpler portions of the image can be saved in the GIF format. Slices in an Illustrator document map to table cells on a web page.

Figure 6–9: A web graphic sliced to create smaller images.

Image Maps

Image maps link one or more areas of an image to a Uniform Resource Locator (URL). The areas of an image map that are linked to a URL are called hotspots. When an image map is used on a web page and a hotspot is clicked, the linked URL is opened in a web browser. In Illustrator, an image map is exported as a single image file, whereas a sliced image is exported as a web page.

The Slice Tool

The **Slice** tool enables you to divide artwork into slices. You can create slices by manually slicing the selected object, using guides to define the slices, or duplicating an existing slice. You can set various options for the **Slice** tool to control slice creation.

Slice Tool Option	Specifies
Slice Type	Whether the slice is an image, standard HTML text on a plain background, or Illustrator text converted to HTML text. The **Image** option converts the slice area to an image file on a web page. The **No Image** option contains HTML text and background color. The **HTML Text** option converts text in an Illustrator document to HTML text with basic formatting.
Name	The name of the slice.
URL	The URL the slice links to.
Target	The area within an HTML document or frame that the slice links to.
Message	The message that is displayed in the browser's status bar during mouse over actions.
Alt	The alternate text that is displayed when an image takes time to load on the web page, or when the image cannot be displayed.
Background	The background color for the slice.

 Note: You can choose to hide or show slices by selecting **View→Hide Slices**.

The Devices Profile

The **Devices** profile is an Illustrator document startup profile that you can use to create artwork for mobile devices. It helps you select the device for which you want to create artwork. Once you select a device, the **Devices** profile automatically provides preset values for the page size and resolution of the document.

 Access the Checklist tile on your CHOICE Course screen for reference information and job aids on How to Create Slices and Image Maps.

ACTIVITY 6-3
Creating Slices and Image Maps

Data File

C:\092034Data\Preparing Content for Deployment\Emerald Epicure Homepage.png

Scenario

Your company is creating a website for Emerald Epicure. The home page is ready and you are now creating other pages in the site. The home page has several images that you want to reuse in your artwork.

1. **Create a new document with the Web profile.**
   a) Select the **New file** button.
   b) From the categories across the top of the **New Document** dialog box, select **Web**.
   c) In the **New Document** dialog box, replace "Untitled-#" with *My Emerald Epicure for the Web*

      The number after **Untitled** varies depending on whether you created other new documents since you started Illustrator.
   d) Set the **Width** to *1280* and **Height** to *800*
   e) Under **Advanced Options**, verify **Color Mode** is set to RGB and **Raster Effects** is set to **Screen (72 ppi)**.
   f) Select **Create** to create a new document with the **Web** profile.

2. **Place the image of the home page within the file.**
   a) Select **File→Place**.
   b) In the **Place** dialog box, navigate to **C:\092034Data\Preparing Content for Deployment**.
   c) Select **Emerald Epicure Homepage.png** and select **Place**.
   d) Click on the artboard to place the graphic.
   e) Magnify the document to **100%**.

3. **Create slices of the image.**
   a) Select the **Web** workspace.
   b) In the **Tools** panel, select the **Slice** tool.
   c) Drag the mouse from the top-left corner of the image in the "The Saga of Olives" section to the bottom-right corner of the image to create a rectangular selection.

d) Observe that red color guides indicate the creation of a slice.

e) Drag the mouse from the top-left corner of the image in the "The History of Olives" section to the bottom-right corner of the image to create a rectangular selection.

f) Similarly, create a slice for the image in the "Cultivation and Harvest" section.

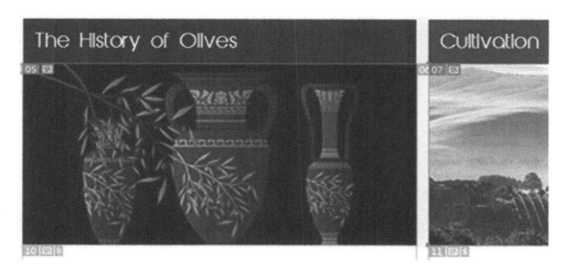

4. Save the slices as images.

a) Select **File→Save Selected Slices**.

b) In the **Save Optimized As** dialog box, navigate to the **C:\092034Data\Preparing Content for Deployment** folder.

c) In the **File name** text box, type *Emerald Epicure Slices* and select **Save**.

d) Select **File→Save As**.

e) Navigate to the **C:\092034Data\Preparing Content for Deployment** folder and save the file as *My Emerald Epicure for the Web.ai*

f) In the **Illustrator Options** dialog box, select **OK**.

g) In the **Tools** panel, select the **Selection** tool to deselect the **Slice Selection** tool.

5. Create an image map.

a) Select **Window→Attributes**.

b) If the **Image Map** section is not displayed, select the **Options** menu and select **Show All** to show additional options.

c) From the **Image Map** drop-down menu, select **Rectangle**.

d) In the **URL** text box, enter *www.emeraldepicure.com*

e) Collapse the **Attributes** panel.

f) Save the file.

TOPIC D

Save Graphics for the Web

You saved an Illustrator graphic as slices for use on a web page. There are various formats for saving web images. One commonly used format is the SVG format. When saving images in the SVG format, it is important to ensure that attributes applied to the image are supported by the format.

In this topic, you will save artwork in the SVG format and save graphics for the web.

SVG

Scalable Vector Graphics (SVG) is an image format that is defined by an open set of specifications developed by the World Wide Web Consortium (W3C). The SVG format is an XML-based format suitable for storing two-dimensional static or dynamic vector graphics. By using the SVG format, you can create interactive web graphics.

The XML files describe the SVG images and their attributes. You can use text editors to create and edit the XML files describing SVG images. Rendering of SVG images is supported by recent versions of web browsers such as Mozilla Firefox®, Microsoft Edge, Google Chrome™, Opera™, and Safari®.

SVG Effects

SVG effects help you add XML-based and resolution-independent effects to objects. Illustrator provides a default set of SVG effects. An SVG effect is defined as a set of XML properties that you can apply to your artwork or edit to create custom effects.

SVG Interactivity

The SVG format supports interactivity by responding to user interaction. As with all interactivity, you can execute a script when an event is detected. The **SVG Interactivity** panel in Illustrator provides an easy way to create interactive SVG graphics by using JavaScript®. You can select an event and enter the JavaScript to be executed when the event is detected. You can use JavaScript for creating specific effects such as rollovers, animations, and drop-down menus.

SVG Events

Illustrator provides many events that can be associated with an SVG image to detect user response.

Event	Executes the Action
onfocusin	When the element receives focus.
onload	After the SVG document is completely parsed by the browser. You can use this event to call one-time-only initialization functions.
onerror	When an element does not load properly or another error occurs.
onabort	When page loading is stopped before the element is completely loaded.
onunload	When the SVG document is removed from a window or frame.
onzoom	When the zoom level is changed for the document.
onresize	When the document is resized in the browser window.
onscroll	When the document is scrolled or panned.

Event	Executes the Action
onfocusout	When an element loses focus.
onactivate	When an element is activated by a mouse click or key press.
onmousedown	When the mouse button is pressed down on an element.
onmouseup	When the mouse button is pressed and then released over an element.
onclick	When the mouse is clicked over an element.
onmouseover	When the mouse pointer is moved onto an element.
onmousemove	While the mouse pointer is over an element.
onmouseout	When the mouse pointer is moved away from an element.
onkeydown	When a key is pressed and held down.
onkeypress	While a key is pressed.
onkeyup	When a key is pressed and released.

The Pixel Preview Mode

The *Pixel Preview* mode enables you to preview the appearance of rasterized graphics. In a rasterized graphic, you can control the size, movement, placement, and anti-aliasing of objects by using the **Pixel Preview** mode. The pixel grid divides the artboard by increments of one pixel. You can view the pixel grid by zooming to 600 percent magnification of the artboard. By using the **Snap to Pixel** property of an object, you can snap an object to the pixel grid.

Extract CSS Properties

You can create the design for an HTML page in Illustrator. This can provide a visual guide for a website developer who can reference the design to code the page layout, styles, and objects into an HTML editor. The problem with doing it that way is that it is a time-consuming and tedious process to replicate the exact appearance and position of all the objects on the page.

With Illustrator, when you create an HTML page, you can also generate and export the underlying Cascading Style Sheet (CSS) code. This allows you to control the appearance of text and objects in the HTML page. You can export the CSS code for individual objects, or for the entire page layout.

 Access the Checklist tile on your CHOICE Course screen for reference information and job aids on How to Save Graphics for the Web.

ACTIVITY 6-4
Saving Graphics for the Web

Before You Begin
The file My Emerald Epicure for the Web.ai is open.

Scenario
Now that your artwork is ready for the web, you want to save it in a suitable format. You want to save the document as an image that can be used as a thumbnail on the Emerald Epicure website.

1. Verify that **My Emerald Epicure for the Web.ai** created in the previous activity is open.

2. Save the document as a **PNG** image.
   a) Select **View→Snap to Grid** to align objects to the pixel grid.
   b) Select **File→Document Color Mode** and verify that **RGB Color** is selected.
   c) Select **File→Export→Save for Web (Legacy)**.
   d) In the **Save for Web** dialog box, in the **Preset** section, from the **Name** drop-down list, select **PNG-24**.

    Note: The **Save for Web & Devices** dialog box in previous versions of Illustrator has been replaced by the **Save for Web** dialog box. Although Adobe labels this box "Legacy," it continues to be popular with web designers. Also, Illustrator does not show previews in Adobe Device Central because technological enhancements in modern mobile devices allow devices to render web pages more effectively.

   e) Select **Save** to save the document in the **PNG** format.
   f) In the **Save Optimized As** dialog box, rename the file as *My-Emerald-Epicure-Web-Graphic* and select **Save**.
   g) Close the file.

TOPIC E

Prepare Documents for Video

You saved graphics in SVG format and for the web. Now you will prepare Illustrator documents for video production. You will learn how to set up a document for video, use layers, insert text, and choose video file formats. In this topic, you will prepare documents for video.

Video Document Setup

Adobe Illustrator is an excellent choice if you want to create graphics for Adobe Premiere® Pro (video editor) or Adobe After Effects® (motion graphics/visual effects/animation editor). It's already vector-based and has a lot of flexibility in its output capabilities.

To save yourself time and headache later, start your new document by choosing the **Film & Video** profile. In the **Size** area, choose what type of video this is for, such as NTSC, PAL, HDTV, Film, and so on. The choice you select will change the values for size, color mode, units, orientation, transparency, and resolution. Illustrator creates only square pixel files. To make sure that the sizes are correctly interpreted by a video editor, Illustrator adjusts the width and height values. For example, if you select the NTSC DV Standard, Illustrator uses a pixel size of 654 × 480. This in turn translates to 740 × 480 pixels in a video-based application. It also puts video-safe guides (Safe Frames) in place to help you lay out your design for optimal viewing. Although Safe Frames are less relevant for web, computers, and mobile devices, they are still required by many broadcast TV companies.

Layers

Video editing programs such as After Effects do not "see" layers the same way Illustrator does. After Effects can see only the top-level layers of an imported Illustrator file. It cannot see the nested layers in the composition timeline, and cannot extract sub-layers.

If you need to animate anything as a separate element, it should be placed in its own top-level layer, and not nested away somewhere. Make sure the layers are well-organized with a clear naming convention. This can save many hours of time for the animator.

Remove all layer effects such as drop shadows, blurs, and glows. Then use the **Release to Layers** command to quickly rearrange nested elements into their own layers. Logically group the layers so that it's easier for the animator to work with them. Be sure to delete any unnecessary or empty layers.

Text and Video

The amount of on-screen text has a critical impact on the timing of a video. A viewer has to have a comfortable amount of time to read and understand the text. Make all text content decisions before the animation/editing begins, as any major changes can potentially disrupt the flow of the video.

Make sure the text is vectorized and scaled large enough for the expected output. For example, an HDTV screen is 1,920 × 1,080 pixels, so bear that in mind when you're considering how large text should appear on the screen. You can always have something scaled larger and then have the video editor scale it down to maintain good resolution. Prefer to use OpenType/TrueType fonts as they are compatible with both Macs and PCs.

If you must use non-standard fonts, make sure they can be exported from Illustrator and imported into the video editing software. You can use the **File packaging** feature or a third party tool to automatically gather and save an Illustrator document's fonts and linked graphics into a single folder. If you have any custom text that won't change, consider using an "Outline Font" so there are no issues with exporting and importing fonts.

Figure 6-10: Text for video.

Video File Formats

The best way to pre-stage your video file formats is to have selected the profile from the beginning. However, if this was not done, find out what the video format expects of the file so that you can make adjustments as necessary. Open a blank document, selecting the **Film & Video** profile. Also select the size such as 4K UHD, 8K FUKD, NTSC, PAL, HDV 720, HDV/HDTV 1080, Film, and more. Observe the dimension, bleed, color modes, raster effects, and the like for that format.

Adobe After Effects and Premiere can import native Illustrator *.ai files (the preferred choice). They can also import most media file formats. If you save the file as a Targa file (*.tga), the artwork is automatically rasterized, which Premiere requires.

It is commonplace for video editing software to use original source files without making its own copy. Make sure you do not modify Illustrator (source) files that are already in use in the video editor. Chances are such changes will not translate well to the video under production. Changing color, or even slightly changing dimensions, position, scale, anchor, rotation, and the like can destroy weeks of careful video editing work.

Guidelines for Preparing Documents for Video Publishing

 Note: All Guidelines for this lesson are available as checklists from the **Checklist** tile on the CHOICE Course screen.

Prepare Documents for Video Publishing

Here are some guidelines for preparing documents for video publishing:

- Files should be in RGB color mode
- If video editing will happen in another Adobe product such as After Effects or Premiere, files should be saved in Illustrator's own **.ai** format, with PDF compatibility turned on.

- Split everything sensibly into separate, smaller, more manageable files, named and organized according to their purpose
- Provide graphics files separately, rather than embedding or linking them, so they can be imported and composited directly into the video editor.
- Save each artboard to a separate file, as your video editor may have trouble with multiple artboards. When you export, select the **Use Artboards** check box.
- Save icons and logos in vector format, or high resolution bitmaps with alpha channels. Make sure the color is RGB.
- Be aware that Premiere Pro will convert a file to a rasterized, bitmapped, pixel-by-pixel graphic.
- Use transparency only to create transparent elements, not lighter colors. If you need to animate transparency, keep the elements at 100 percent opacity and let the animator change the opacity during video editing.

ACTIVITY 6–5
Preparing Documents for Video

Scenario

The video production department has asked your design team to provide some content for the next television commercial spot. Management wants to make sure that all team members understand what is required for preparing Illustrator documents for video. They have asked you to explain some of the key points. Discuss the following questions.

1. Under what conditions would Safe Frames be useful or required?

2. What must you do to an Illustrator document that has layers before importing it into Adobe After Effects?

3. What are some issues with regard to including text in video that the design team must be aware of?

4. What is the best way to select the correct video output file format?

TOPIC F

Prepare Files for Other Applications

You have prepared Illustrator documents for print, web, and video. You will now learn to prepare files for other applications such as Microsoft® Office. You will learn how to preserve layers and set color settings.

File Format

Many Adobe applications are designed to work with each other. Illustrator makes it particularly easy to transfer vector files to Adobe Photoshop®, InDesign®, and Animate®. In fact, Illustrator artwork can import directly into the Animate environment, or directly into Flash Player. Illustrator offers you several save options, such as an EPS, which works for Photoshop and InDesign; PDF, which is best for emailing and viewing on screen; and SVG, which is the best format for animation and video software, such as Animate and After Effects.

Other Applications

Microsoft Office is a suite of commonly used programs. Although native Illustrator files do not directly transfer over to Office documents, they can be saved into common image formats such as JPG, GIF, PNG, and so on by selecting **File→Export→Export As**. They can also be converted into an encapsulated PostScript (EPS). To do this simply open the Illustrator file and select **File→Save a Copy**. From the **File Type** drop-down list, select **Illustrator EPS** and then select **Save**. You will then be able to insert the image into Microsoft Word, PowerPoint®, Excel® and other applications.

Preserve Illustrator Layers

Because Adobe programs are meant to work with each other, you are able to preserve layers when exporting into another program such as Photoshop. To export an Illustrator file to Photoshop, select **File→Export→Export As** and from the **Save As** drop-down menu, select **Photoshop (PSD)**. Then select **Export**. This will bring up the **Photoshop Export Options** dialog box. From here you can change settings such as resolution and color model. To ensure that the layers are preserved, select the **Write Layers** option.

 Access the Checklist tile on your CHOICE Course screen for reference information and job aids on How to **Prepare Files for Other Applications.**

ACTIVITY 6-6
Preparing a File for Use in Other Adobe Applications

Data File

C:\092034Data\Preparing Content for Deployment\Emerald Epicure.ai

Scenario

You decide that you want to do some editing in Photoshop. To do this, you need to save the file in the correct format. In addition, there is going to be a presentation done in Microsoft PowerPoint, showcasing all of the Emerald Epicure campaign materials. You will also need to save a file that is appropriate for Microsoft Office.

---

1. Open **C:\092034Data\Preparing Content for Deployment\Emerald Epiciure.ai.**

2. If necessary, select **Close** to accept the missing font substitutions.

3. Save the Emerald Epicure file for Photoshop.
   a) Go to **File→Export→Export As**.
   b) From the **Save as type** drop-down list, select **Photoshop (*.PSD)**.
   c) Select **Export**.
   d) In the **Photoshop Export Options** dialog box, from the **Color Model** drop-down list, select **RGB**.
   e) Change the **Resolution** to **Screen (72 ppi)**.
   f) Select **OK**.

4. Save the Emerald Epicure file to use in Microsoft PowerPoint.
   a) Go to **File→Export→Export As**.
   b) From the **Save as type** drop-down list, select **PNG (*.PNG)**.
   c) Check **Use Artboards** and verify that **All** is selected to save each artboard as a separate file.
   d) Select **Export**.
   e) In the **PNG Options** dialog box, accept the default settings and select **OK**.
   f) If a warning message is displayed, review the message and then select **OK**.

5. Close all open documents.

Summary

In this lesson, you prepared your content for deployment. You prepared artwork and colors for printing, set up graphics for the web, and set up documents to contain video. You then saved and exported your documents in different file formats for other applications.

Imagine using Illustrator to create artwork for your website. What features will you find most useful to assist you for this task?

Suppose you created artwork for commercial printing. What settings and features will you apply to convert the artwork to graphics optimized for the web?

 Note: Check your CHOICE Course screen for opportunities to interact with your classmates, peers, and the larger CHOICE online community about the topics covered in this course or other topics you are interested in. From the Course screen you can also access available resources for a more continuous learning experience.

7 | Setting Project Requirements

Lesson Time: 30 minutes

Lesson Introduction

As a designer and developer using Adobe® Illustrator®, you will need to have a solid understanding of the purpose and audience for rich media content. You will need to identify project requirements, client goals, audience needs, and common problems that arise throughout the project development cycles. You will also need to be familiar with the term intellectual property. Finally, you will need to have a solid understanding of project tasks and common problems that arise throughout the project development cycle. In this lesson, you will set project requirements.

Lesson Objectives

In this lesson, you will:

- Identify purpose, audience, and audience needs.

- Identify and adhere to established copyright rules.

- Determine project management tasks.

TOPIC A

Identify the Purpose, Audience, and Audience Needs

As an Adobe Illustrator designer and developer, you will need to have a solid understanding of the purpose and audience for rich media content. You will need to identify client goals, your audience, and the needs of your audience.

In this topic, you will learn how to identify the purpose of the project, determine client requirements and goals, and identify your audience and its needs.

Purpose

When determining the purpose of the content, it is necessary to consider the client's goals for the project, and identify how the rich media content can best fulfill those goals. Is the purpose to educate, entertain, or inform? What types of media, functionality, and interactivity will be needed?

Audience

In identifying how the rich media content should be communicated, it's important to consider the demographics of the target audience. Key demographics generally include age group, gender, computer literacy, education, income level, and geographical location. How relevant the demographics will be to a project will vary from project to project.

Audience Needs

What does your audience expect to gain from the experience, and how can you best meet their needs? Consider usability, accessibility, engagement, and what technology the audience will be using to determine how audience needs can best be met.

Guidelines for Identifying the Purpose, Audience, and Audience Needs

 Note: All Guidelines for this lesson are available as checklists from the **Checklist** tile on the CHOICE Course screen.

Here are some guidelines for identifying project purpose, audience, and audience needs.

Determine the Project Purpose and Objectives

Identify the following:

* What should be the final outcome of the project? Is it a call to action, such as prompting donations for a nonprofit organization? Boosting book sales? Or is it informational, such as an instructional video, or pamphlet?

Determine Your Audience

Identify the following:

* Age range
* Gender
* Education level

- Socioeconomic class

Determine Your Audience Needs

Identify the following:

- If you are designing for a specific audience, what would appeal to them?
- What challenges or constraints are they facing? For instance, if you are designing for college students, you would realize that the majority of them face financial burdens.

ACTIVITY 7–1
Determining Your Target Audience

Data Files

C:\092034Data\Setting Project Requirements\chocolates.png

C:\092034Data\Setting Project Requirements\zoo.png

C:\092034Data\Setting Project Requirements\billboard.png

C:\092034Data\Setting Project Requirements\business_card.png

Scenario

Most design projects are created with the target audience in mind, the designer implementing design elements specific to the demographics within that audience. Examine the files and determine the target audience for each one of them. This is an open discussion. There are no right or wrong answers. Be sure to share your opinion, especially if it is different from others. You may have experiences or a different perspective that can add value to the conversation.

---

1. Open **C:\092034Data\Setting Project Requirements\chocolates.png** and answer the following questions.

2. What is the target audience demographic, such as age, gender, profession, and so on?

3. In what type of environment would the product be most successful?

4. Is the finished design effective in reaching its target audience?

5. Open the website **ww5.komen.org** and answer the following questions.

6. What is the target audience?

7. What is the objective of the website?

8. Open the **C:\092034Data\Setting Project Requirements\zoo.png** file and answer the following questions.

9. What is the target audience?

10. Which elements present in the design lead you to that conclusion?

11. Open the C:\092034Data\Setting Project Requirements\billboard.png file and answer the following questions.

12. What is the target audience?

13. Given the client, is this an effective way to advertise their product?

14. Is it evident that this is an attempt at reaching a new demographic?

15. Open the C:\092034Data\Setting Project Requirements\business_card.png file and answer the following questions.

16. What is the target audience?

17. Which elements present in the design lead you to that conclusion?

18. What about this particular design makes it somewhat different from the previous designs?

19. Close all open files without saving changes.

TOPIC B

Determine and Evaluate Standard Copyright Rules for Artwork, Graphics, and Graphics Use

All products resulting from human creativity are considered intellectual property. Copyright law, developed to protect intellectual property, was enacted to enable our society to progress. Because you create original work when you build web pages and you might use graphics, illustrations, and text created by others in building those pages, you are on both sides of the copyright law. As a web page creator, you seek both protection for your intellectual property and fair and legal use of the intellectual property of others.

A copyright is protection of a specific and tangible expression of an idea. It does not protect the idea. That expression can take the form of a novel, song, design, movie, website, and so on. A trademark is similar but it protects a design, image, slogan, symbol, or word that identifies goods or services. The copyright owner obtains the copyright at the moment of realization or completion of the tangible result from the idea.

Copyrighted Material

One limitation to the copyright law is for fair use. Fair use allows limited use of a copyright-protected work. What is allowable is determined by the following factors:

- The purpose of the use
- The nature of the copyright-protected work
- How much is to be copied
- The effect on the market or value of the work

Fair use is determined on a case-by-case basis. It is in common use for commentary, criticism, library archiving, news reporting, research, scholarship, and teaching.

If you will be using text or graphics owned by others, you should properly cite the origin of the information. This should be done whether the copyright symbol or notice is present in the original or not.

If you suspect a work is copyrighted, seek out the owner and request permission to use all or part of the work. Many websites have sufficient contact information. If you believe the copyright is recorded at the U.S. Copyright Office and it was recorded after 1978, you can research the owner online at **www.copyright.gov**. Copyrights recorded before 1978 can be researched by their staff for a fee.

Copyrighted Source Material

The primary way to identify copyrighted material is by checking for a copyright notice. However, you can no longer depend on this notice being present. The use of a copyright notice was once required as a condition of copyright protection, but it is now optional. The notice does not register the copyright with the U.S. Copyright Office. If you wish to register a copyright you must do it through that office.

It is a good idea to put a copyright notice on your website so visitors are reminded that your site is protected by copyright. The general form of the notice is **"Copyright 2018 The Emerald Epicure Ltd. All Rights Reserved."** The copyright symbol © may be substituted for the word **"Copyright."**

Guidelines for Determining and Evaluating Standard Copyright Rules for Artwork, Graphics, and Graphics Use

Determine and Evaluate Standard Copyright Rules for Artwork, Graphics, and Graphics Use

To determine whether or not an element is valid for reproduction and use, ask yourself the following questions:

- Did I create it?
  - If so, you may use it for whatever you like. You might also want to consider obtaining your own copyright for the image.
  - If not, find out who did and obtain permission from them. If this is not possible, do not use the image in question.
- Did I pay for it?
  - There are many sites on which you can obtain free-to-use graphics and/or photographs. Some are even free for download. However, if you are using images from one of these sites, be sure to check the owner's specifications on usage. In some cases they are free only for personal use and not commercial use.
- What am I going to do with it?
  - If it is for student use, you are generally free to use it for a project. However, if it is for commercial purposes, it is vital that you obtain permission from the author so that you don't end up in court.
  - There is such a thing as Fair-Use, which allows the designer to use the image for educating, research, parodies, and critiques, as long as its value is not compromised.
  - Altering someone else's image does not change ownership, even if it is up to 99 percent altered. In some cases, the court has found that artwork has not infringed upon copyright laws because the original image was no longer recognizable. This is not always the case and is not a law.
- Where did I get the image?
  - Did you find the image on the Internet? Some people believe that the Internet is public domain, but this is not the case.
  - If it is an image scanned from print, it is still subject to all copyright laws.
- Is the image in question?
  - If the image is in question, just don't use it.
  - It's not worth a lawsuit or the damage it can have on your professional reputation.
  - With enough work and training, chances are you can create something similar, eliminating any concern over violating copyright laws.

ACTIVITY 7-2
Reviewing Copyright and Citation Principles

Before You Begin

Review the following situations and determine whether or not you should use the image.

Scenario

Emerald Epicure's marketing department has ideas about a new look for its campaign materials. In a meeting, they showed you mock-ups of web pages, posters, and brochures that they would like you to develop. You noticed that some of the content looks like it was downloaded from the Internet. You asked them if they are aware of copyright restrictions regarding using images. The marketing department manager has asked you to clarify to the team when it is permissible to use multimedia content.

1. In terms of licensing, can you use a photograph that you took yourself?

2. In terms of licensing, can you use another group's logo on a website that contains references to that group such as its products or services?

3. In terms of licensing, can you use an image found on the Internet?

4. In terms of licensing, can you use a royalty-free image downloaded for free?

5. In terms of licensing, can you use a royalty-free image paid for on a stock photography site?

6. In terms of licensing, can you use a video downloaded from the Internet?

TOPIC C

Determine and Evaluate Project Management Tasks and Responsibilities

As an Adobe Illustrator designer and developer, you will need to have a solid understanding of project tasks and common problems that arise throughout the project development cycle.

In this topic, you will learn how to identify components of a project plan and life cycle, as well as the importance of receiving feedback on your design plans.

Items on a Project Plan

The objective of a project plan is to identify the approach that the project team will use to produce and deliver the scope of the project. A well-planned project ensures that the project meets specific objectives within the given time frame, and helps streamline the development process. At minimum, the project plan answers these four questions:

- Why is there a need for the project?
- What is the work that will be performed?
- Who will be involved and what will their responsibilities be?
- When will the project be delivered?

The following table defines some of the items that generally appear within a project plan.

Component	Description
Project scope	Detail specifications, internal due dates, milestones for project deliverables that the client would then approve, and final deadlines.
Tasks	A list of items that need to be accomplished in order to meet the project milestones.
Due dates	Due dates include internal deadlines for tasks and project phases, as well as due dates for client deliverables.
Resource allocation	Indicates which tasks go to which team members.

Project Plan Phases

A project phase can be thought of as a project life cycle that typically goes through five different cycles. A typical process might begin with defining the project goals, expectations, and audience. The next phase includes designing the framework of the project. Once the foundation has been laid, the development begins, followed by testing, revisions, and client approval. The last phase is the final launch. Breaking a project down into manageable, sequential phases with definitions and deliverables for each helps keep the project organized and on track.

Component	Description
Planning and analysis	Initial project planning begins.
	Client goals and expectations are established.
	Target audience needs are identified.

Component	Description
Designing	Style guides and color schemes are created.
	Wireframes are built.
	Initial designs are mocked up.
Building/Development	Interactivity and functionality are developed.
	Graphics are integrated.
Testing	Quality assurance performs usability tests.
	Any issues, bugs, and errors are reported back to the design and development teams for revision.
Implementing	All issues that arose from testing are fixed.
	Client has given approval to launch the final product.

mockup ⟵ (handwritten annotation)

Feedback on Design Plans

Feedback is crucial to improving the user experience because it tells you how effective your project is in the eyes of those who are using it. Lack of feedback is like walking through a dark forest without a flashlight.

A developer can become so focused on creating the components and functionality of a design that he can't envision how a user might respond to the overall experience. Good sources of feedback are peers and clients. Before sending for client review, it is good practice to have an internal review and gain feedback from peers. Revise based on peer feedback, then send for client feedback and revise again as needed.

Guidelines for Determining and Evaluating Project Management Tasks and Responsibilities

Determine and Evaluate Project Management Tasks and Responsibilities

Follow these guidelines to determine and evaluate project management tasks and responsibilities.

- Project Life Cycle
  - Initiation
    - Project is defined
  - Planning and Analysis
    1. Objectives are decided upon
    2. Intended audience is discovered
    3. Items that should be ready for output are discussed
    4. Available assets
    5. Resources
    6. Tasks are assigned within the group
  - Building
    - Product or service is developed
  - Monitoring
    - Overseeing of project to ensure punctual delivery
  - Closing
    - Project is wrapped up

- Project Management
    - Avoid common issues such as objectives or responsibilities not being well-defined.
    - Ensure that delivery plan is acceptable to clients and key stakeholders.
    - Set standards from the beginning and ensure that they are being adhered to.
    - Ensure proper communication is being practiced at all times.
    - Delegate specific tasks according to team members' strengths.

ACTIVITY 7-3

Determining and Evaluating Project Management Tasks and Responsibilities

Scenario

Emerald Epicure's marketing department would like to begin a new campaign to launch a new product. This campaign will include marketing materials such as a new area on their existing site, new posters, a new logo, and new promotional videos. You will also be working with new team members as the team leader, a responsibility that is new to you.

---

1. What are the project plan phases? How will they apply to this particular project and its objectives?

2. Your team consists of six people, including you. How will you go about dividing up the tasks?

3. How will you, as team leader, ensure that you meet the deadline, as well as the project objectives?

Summary

In this lesson, you learned about setting project requirements. You learned how to identify an audience and its needs. You also learned about copyright rules and project management tasks associated with creative project development.

What do you think will be the biggest challenge in identifying your audience's needs?

Why do you think that it is very important to get timely feedback on design plans?

 Note: Check your CHOICE Course screen for opportunities to interact with your classmates, peers, and the larger CHOICE online community about the topics covered in this course or other topics you are interested in. From the Course screen you can also access available resources for a more continuous learning experience.

Course Follow-Up

Congratulations! You have completed the *Adobe® Illustrator® CC: Part 2* course. In this course, you created complex illustrations, enhanced artwork using painting tools, managed colors, formatted type, enhanced the appearance of artwork, prepared artwork for commercial printing, and generated graphics for the web. You can now create complex illustrations using advanced tools, options, and effects. In addition, you are able to prepare artwork for print output and graphics for the web.

What's Next?

This is the last course in the Adobe® Illustrator® series. You can take related media/web development-related Logical Operations courses, such as those in the Adobe® InDesign® series, to further enhance your knowledge.

You are encouraged to explore Illustrator further by actively participating in any of the social media forums set up by your instructor or training administrator through the **Social Media** tile on the CHOICE Course screen.

A Mapping Course Content to Adobe Certified Professional in Graphic Design & Illustration Using Adobe Illustrator Exam

Currently, through **Certiport.com**, Adobe offers the Adobe Certified Professional certification program. Candidates who wish to obtain Illustrator certification must pass the associated exam.

To assist you in your preparation for the exam, Logical Operations has provided a reference document that indicates where the current exam objectives are covered in the Logical Operations *Adobe® Illustrator® CC* courseware.

The exam-mapping document is available from the **Course** page on CHOICE. Log on to your CHOICE account, select the tile for this course, select the **Files** tile, and download and unzip the course files. The mapping reference will be in a subfolder named **Mappings**.

Best of luck in your exam preparation!

Mastery Builders

Mastery Builders are provided for certain lessons as additional learning resources for this course. Mastery Builders are developed for selected lessons within a course in cases when they seem most instructionally useful as well as technically feasible. In general, Mastery Builders are supplemental, optional unguided practice and may or may not be performed as part of the classroom activities. Your instructor will consider setup requirements, classroom timing, and instructional needs to determine which Mastery Builders are appropriate for you to perform, and at what point during the class. If you do not perform the Mastery Builders in class, your instructor can tell you if you can perform them independently as self-study, and if there are any special setup requirements.

Mastery Builder 1–1
Creating Complex Illustrations

Activity Time: 15 minutes

Scenario

You have been working on a product brochure for Emerald Epicure. You have been asked to create a white bottle on a blue background that will be taller than the bottle in the green brochure. You have in mind something like this:

---

1. Create a new **Print** document. In the **New Document** box, name the document *Bottle on Blue Background*. Set the **dimensions** to *1280* by *800* Points, with just one artboard.

2. Create a large blue rectangle to serve as the background. Name the layer which contains this rectangle *Blue Background*

3. Create a new **layer** and name it *Bottle*

4. Draw a rounded rectangle to serve as the body of the bottle. Pull the bottom right and left selection handles inward slightly.

5. Create a copy of the rounded rectangle. Resize it to slightly smaller than the bottle. Place it within the bottle and unite the two by cutting out the inner shape.

 Note: Use the **Pathfinder** panel.

6. Draw a rectangle to serve as the top of the bottle. Merge it with the main body of the bottle.

7. Draw a rectangle to serve as the bottle stopper. Pull the bottom right and left selection handles inward slightly. Place it above the bottle.

8. Use the **Pencil** tool to draw the drop of oil and the shadow at the base of the bottle.

9. Save the file as *My Bottle on Blue Background* and close the file.

Mastery Builder 2–1
Painting Artwork

Activity Time: 15 minutes

Data File
C:\092034Data\Enhancing Artwork Using Painting Tools\Products Brochure.ai

Scenario
You want to enhance the appearance of the front and back covers of your brochure. You feel that adding a shadow for the oil container, creating a background for the cover, painting the objects, and drawing appealing paths will help enhance the brochure.

---

1. Open **C:\092034Data\Enhancing Artwork Using Painting Tools \Products Brochure.ai**.

2. Using the **Blob Brush** tool, create a gray color shadow at the base of the oil bottle.

3. On the right artboard, select the set of paths and rectangles on top of the blue rectangle and create a **Live Paint** group.

 Note: Hint: Use Object→Live Paint→Make.

4. Using the **Live Paint Selection** tool, apply alternating dark and light blue colors to the different faces of the Live Paint group.

5. Select the blue triangle at the top of the page and use it to create a scatter brush. Remove the triangle you used for creating the scatter brush from the artboard.

6. Using the **Scatter** brush, create a curved path starting from the top-left corner of the Live Paint group. Continue painting the path by moving upward and then downward, touching the Live Paint group.

7. Create another curved path to extend the curved path that lies within the Live Paint group and fill it with white color. On the front cover of the brochure, create a dark blue rectangle in the **Background_1 layer**.

8. Change the stroke color of the oil container to **None**.

9. Create a mesh on the background rectangle and adjust the mesh points so that the bottle appears to have a light glow behind it and the corners of the background appear darker.

10. Save the file as *My Products Brochure.ai* and close the file.

Mastery Builder 3–1
Applying Colors Using Custom Swatches

Activity Time: 15 minutes

Data File
C:\092034Data\Customizing Colors and Swatches\Products Brochure.ai

Scenario
The back cover of the brochure is empty except for a patterned border at the bottom. You want to make it more appealing by adding colors to the background.

---

1. Open **C:\092034Data\Customizing Colors and Swatches\Products Brochure.ai**. If necessary, close the missing fonts message.

2. Create a rectangle with a width of **6** inches and a height of **4.5** inches. Position it at the top-left of the back cover of the brochure on the left artboard.

3. Create a new swatch named *My Swatch* and set the CMYK values to **97, 70, 25**, and **7**, respectively. Apply it to the rectangle you created.

4. From the **Analogous 2 Harmony Rule**, select the last seven colors in the second row and save them as a color group in the **Swatches** panel.

5. Create another rectangle with a width of **6** inches and a height of **3.85** inches. Position it at the bottom-half of the page.

6. Fill the rectangle with the third color (blue) from the color group you added to the **Swatches** panel. Set the opacity to **70%**.

7. From the **PANTONE+ CMYK Uncoated** color library, add the first color (cyan) in the first row to the **Swatches** panel.

    Note: Use the Color Books library.

8. Navigate to the folder **C:\092034Data\Customizing Colors and Swatches** and save the file as *My Products Brochure.ai*

9. Close the file.

Mastery Builder 4–1
Formatting Text in an Illustrator Document

Activity Time: 15 minutes

Data File

C:\092034Data\Formatting Type\Products Brochure.ai

Scenario

You added all the necessary elements to the brochure except the product descriptions. You want to add and format the product descriptions to enhance their appearance and readability. Also, you want to add the company name to the front cover of the brochure and format the company name on the back cover.

---

1. Open **C:\092034Data\Formatting Type\Products Brochure.ai**. If necessary, close the missing fonts message.

2. Type *Emerald Epicure* above the oil container.

3. Set the fill color of the text to **white**, the font family to **Calibri**, font size to **48 pt**, and font style to **Bold**.

4. On the back cover of the brochure, select the company name in the "CONTACT US" section. Confirm font family is set to **AGaramond Pro** and the font style is set to **Regular**. In the **OpenType** panel, apply the **Stylistic Alternates** formatting.

5. Select artboard 2. Using "Pure Olive Oil" as a heading, type the text *A combination of virgin and light olive oil, Emerald Epicure's Pure Olive Oil gives your food just the right amount of flavor straight from our olive groves.*

6. Select the text you typed, set the font family to **Calibri**, font style to **Regular**, and font size to **12 pt**. Apply white fill and no stroke to the text you typed.

7. Add **5 pt** space before the paragraph.

8. Under "White Truffle Oil," type the text *Drizzle Emerald Epicure's White Truffle Olive Oil over your pastas and risottos and enjoy the aroma of white truffles.*

9. Apply the same character and paragraph formats to this text that you applied to the text in the "Pure Olive Oil" section.

10. Save the file as *My Products Brochure.ai*

11.Close the file.

Mastery Builder 5-1
Enhancing Artwork

Activity Time: 15 minutes

Data Files

C:\092034Data\Enhancing the Appearance of Artwork\Pure.png

C:\092034Data\Enhancing the Appearance of Artwork\White Truffle.png

C:\092034Data\Enhancing the Appearance of Artwork\Products Brochure.ai

Scenario

You added all the product descriptions for your brochure. Now you want to add relevant images for the products. You also want to enhance the appearance of these images by shaping their corners and adding shadows. In addition, you would like to add a decorative pattern in different locations in the brochure.

1. Open **C:\092034Data\Enhancing the Appearance of Artwork\Products Brochure.ai**. If necessary, close the missing fonts message.

2. Create a layer named *Images*

3. From the **C:\092034Data\Enhancing the Appearance of Artwork** folder, place the **Pure.png** and **White Truffle.png** images next to the "Pure Olive Oil" and "White Truffle Oil" product descriptions, respectively, on artboard 2.

4. Create a rounded square with a width and height of **1.5** inches by using white fill and stroke color.

5. Position the rounded rectangle over the image in the "Pure Olive Oil" section.

6. Select the rounded rectangle and the image and create a clipping mask.

7. Similarly, create a clipping mask for the image in the "White Truffle Oil" section.

8. Apply a drop shadow to both the clipping masks by setting **X Offset** to 0.1 in, **Y Offset** to 0.1 in, and **Blur** to 0.07.

9. Select the flower just below the text "Olives and Our Lives."

10. Create a graphic symbol out of the flower you selected and name the symbol *Blue Flower*

11.Place an instance of the symbol on the document and move it to the front cover of the brochure in the space between the oil container and the title "Emerald Epicure." Resize the symbol instance to about half its original size.

12.Save the file as *My Products Brochure.ai* in the C:\092034Data \Enhancing the Appearance of Artwork folder.

13.Close the file.

Mastery Builder 6–1
Setting Print Options

Activity Time: 20 minutes

Data File

C:\092034Data\Preparing Content for Deployment\Emerald Epicure.ai

Scenario

The Emerald Epicure brochure is just about done and ready for printing. Before sending the file to the printer, you want to check it for spelling errors, prepare transparent areas, and rasterize the artwork.

---

1. Open **C:\092034Data\Preparing Content for Deployment\Emerald Epicure.ai**. Close the message to accept the missing fonts.

2. Check the spelling to ensure there are no errors. Fix errors if necessary.

3. Use the **Flattener Preview** option to prepare any transparent areas of the file.

4. Rasterize artwork during printing, if necessary, for gradients, meshes, and more.

5. Set up the **Print** options for multiple artboards, if necessary.

6. Print the file.

7. Make any adjustments where necessary and print again.

8. Close the file without saving your changes.

Mastery Builder 7–1
Setting Project Requirements

Activity Time: 20 minutes

Scenario

You have been hired to begin a new campaign for Emerald Epicure for the launching of a new olive oil product. Before beginning the actual design phase, you must set the project requirements. These questions require much thought, always keeping in mind the client, audience, deadlines, and the desired final outcome.

---

1. What is the purpose of the new campaign?

2. Who is the audience?

3. What are the audience needs?

4. How much of this work will concern the use of copyrighted material?

5. Regarding project planning, consider the following questions.
   a) Why is there a need for the project?
   b) What is the work that will be performed?
   c) Who will be involved and what will their responsibilities be?
   d) When will the project be delivered?

6. What are the project plan phases?

7. How and when will you set a time for receiving project feedback?

Solutions

ACTIVITY 3–4: Adjusting Color

8. Are the results of the Invert and the Complement commands exactly the same?

   A: No, even though they look very close. The inverse is #9642B9, and the complement is #9A45BD.

ACTIVITY 6–5: Preparing Documents for Video

1. Under what conditions would Safe Frames be useful or required?

   A: Answers will vary. Many television broadcast companies still require Safe Frames on a video to ensure that the important parts of the image remain visible to the viewer. Safe Frames are not very relevant on platforms that do not automatically crop the image, such as a computer monitor.

2. What must you do to an Illustrator document that has layers before importing it into Adobe After Effects?

   A: Answers will vary. Because After Effects does not "see" beyond top-level layers, any nested layers must be reorganized as top-level layers. In addition, remove any layer effects, and use naming conventions that are intuitive for the After Effects animators.

3. What are some issues with regard to including text in video that the design team must be aware of?

   A: Answers will vary. Text must be on the screen long enough for the viewer to comfortably read it. Text must be vectorized and scaled large enough for the expected output. Use OpenType/TrueType fonts for maximum compatibility, but if you must use non-standard fonts, then export them from Illustrator and include them in the Illustrator file packaging.

4. What is the best way to select the correct video output file format?

   A: Answers will vary, but most should agree that it is best to pre-stage the video output file format by selecting the correct **Film & Video** profile at the beginning of the project.

ACTIVITY 7-1: Determining Your Target Audience

2. **What is the target audience demographic, such as age, gender, profession, and so on?**

   A: Answers will vary. Some will say that the adult professional woman is the target. Others might expand the gender to both sexes, or place the age at mid-30s–50s.

3. **In what type of environment would the product be most successful?**

   A: Answers will vary. Some will suggest that an upscale boutique shop would be an excellent venue. Others might say online or in a coffee shop.

4. **Is the finished design effective in reaching its target audience?**

   A: Answers will vary, but the consensus will probably be yes.

6. **What is the target audience?**

   A: Answers will vary. Some will say women of all demographic types and ages. Others will say it also includes men, even though that is not obvious in the images. Still others will say anyone who is concerned with finding a cure for breast cancer.

7. **What is the objective of the website?**

   A: Answers will vary. Some will point to the fund-raising aspect. Others will highlight the informational aspect or the effort at building a community.

9. **What is the target audience?**

   A: Answers will vary. Some will say the parents of kids. Others will say the kids themselves.

10. **Which elements present in the design lead you to that conclusion?**

    A: Answers will vary. Those who say the target is parents will point out that the phone number and web address point to an older audience. Others will say the headline of feeding a giraffe would be especially exciting to children.

12. **What is the target audience?**

    A: Answers will vary. Most will say women in their 20s and 30s.

13. **Given the client, is this an effective way to advertise their product?**

    A: Answers will vary. Some students may remember seeing advertising by GAP NOW. People will have different opinions about the effectiveness of this approach. Some will say that it suggests that the target audience wants to differentiate themselves from past generations and, therefore, the approach is effective.

14. **Is it evident that this is an attempt at reaching a new demographic?**

    A: Answers will vary. Some will point out that the color and makeup of the subjects on the left make the images look older, more artificial, and dated (That was then...). The "This is now." images are brighter in color, more vibrant, closer, and more intimate. Some will say it is a new demographic (generation). Others will say it's the same demographic that is re-inventing itself culturally.

16. **What is the target audience?**

    A: Answers will vary, but many will say a slightly younger crowd looking for "edgier" tattoo designs.

17. Which elements present in the design lead you to that conclusion?

A: Answers will vary. The designs are atypical, with more unusual colors. The background is black, which suggests a younger crowd.

18. What about this particular design makes it somewhat different from the previous designs?

A: Answers will vary. The images are "darker" in emotional tone and more fanciful and fantasy-oriented.

ACTIVITY 7–2: Reviewing Copyright and Citation Principles

1. In terms of licensing, can you use a photograph that you took yourself?

A: Yes. These are free to use for whatever you may choose. However, you might want to obtain permission from any subjects in your photographs before using publicly and/or commercially. Many organizations, including governmental, require that the subjects of photos sign a consent to use form.

2. In terms of licensing, can you use another group's logo on a website that contains references to that group such as its products or services?

A: It depends. Logos fall into a kind of a "gray area" because they are considered creative objects, but not always creative enough to warrant copyright protection. Many large corporations have logo-use standards and specifications on their website, as well as a way to contact someone concerning its use.

3. In terms of licensing, can you use an image found on the Internet?

A: No. Unless specifically stated, this is not eligible for free use or reproduction.

4. In terms of licensing, can you use a royalty-free image downloaded for free?

A: Yes. However, although the image is royalty-free, meaning the copyright owner does not require payment or even notification when the image is used, it is not necessarily open for use in any environment. Most images come with specifications for their allotted uses.

5. In terms of licensing, can you use a royalty-free image paid for on a stock photography site?

A: Yes. In most cases, once an image is paid for, you can use it for whatever you may choose. However, many stock image sites have specific licensing terms that you should become familiar with before using one of their images.

6. In terms of licensing, can you use a video downloaded from the Internet?

A: Probably not. Most likely, this video is not safe for use. Many free video sites where people upload their own videos have specific copyright ownership for all videos posted there. As with stock photography, there are also some free stock video sites available for your use.

ACTIVITY 7-3: Determining and Evaluating Project Management Tasks and Responsibilities

1. **What are the project plan phases? How will they apply to this particular project and its objectives?**

   A: Answers will vary. The phases are planning and analysis, designing, building/ development, testing, and implementing. Since this is a product launch, it will greatly impact the company. Many people will be working on it. Timelines and budgets must be met, so a clear project management methodology will be required.

2. **Your team consists of six people, including you. How will you go about dividing up the tasks?**

   A: Answers will vary. The most common way is to assign people to take on tasks they are most suited for. Or, you can allow team members to volunteer to take on certain tasks. The key is to make sure everyone is effectively utilized.

3. **How will you, as team leader, ensure that you meet the deadline, as well as the project objectives?**

   A: Answers will vary. Setting milestones and getting regular feedback from the team and the client are all crucial to the success of any project.

Glossary

anti-aliasing
A technique that smooths jagged edges of text to improve its appearance and readability.

blending mode
A mode that determines how the color of the selected object blends with the color of another object in the underlying layer.

Blob Brush tool
A tool used to draw objects that are filled and have no stroke.

Brushes panel
A panel that displays brushes and enables you to customize and manage the brushes.

clipping mask
An object or set of objects that is used to show and hide artwork based on its outlines.

color group
A group of related solid colors.

color model
A model that generates a range of colors by using combinations of base colors represented as numerical values.

color separation
A process by which four plates, one each for the four process colors, are created for printing a document.

Color Themes panel
A panel that enables you to create color themes or select a color theme created by professional graphic designers and shared online.

composite
A proof of the artwork that is printed to verify the reproduction of colors in the artwork.

compound paths
A way of combining objects by cutting out one object from another.

compound shapes
A way of combining objects by creating a complex shape out of two or more objects.

effect
An appearance attribute that can be applied to an object, a group, or a layer without affecting its structure.

flattening
A process that Illustrator performs to prepare transparent artwork for printing. This process also occurs when saving or exporting artwork to file formats that do not support transparency.

freeform gradient
A type of gradient that provides a graduated blend of color in an ordered or random sequence.

gradient
A coloration technique that transitions from one color to another in a given direction.

Graphic Styles library
A collection of preset or user-defined graphic styles.

grid
A set of evenly spaced horizontal and vertical lines that helps align objects to the nearest pixel and appears at the background of artwork.

guides
Reference lines dragged from the horizontal or vertical ruler that are used to align text and objects.

halftone
The simulation of continuous tones using dots of varying size and spacing in a printed image.

Illustrator effect
An effect that you can apply only to vector graphics.

image map
An image with areas called hotspots, which are linked to a URL.

Image Trace
A command that is used to create a vector illustration based on a raster graphic.

Info panel
A panel that displays information such as the dimension, position, or characteristics of an object, a tool, or a document.

Isolation mode
A mode that isolates a layer, a sublayer, a path, or groups of objects for editing without affecting other objects.

knockout
A technique that is used to prevent a dark underlying color from affecting a light overlapping color when printed.

layer
A placeholder that helps you organize objects and edit them without affecting the other objects in a document.

Live Paint Bucket tool
A tool that uses the currently selected fill and stroke colors to paint the faces and edges of Live Paint groups.

Live Paint group
A set of editable paths that divide a drawing into faces and edges that can be individually filled or stroked.

mesh
A collection of grid lines that controls the flow and transition of multiple colors across an object.

Navigator panel
A panel that highlights the currently visible area of your document and enables you to access the required area in your document.

opacity
A property that when applied to an object, a group of objects, or a layer enables you to see through objects to view objects lying beneath.

opacity mask
An object that is used to show and hide an image that is below it, by varying its transparency.

overprinting
A printing technique that is used to prevent knockouts while printing overlapping colors.

Pathfinder effects
A way of combining objects through interactions among overlapping objects.

pattern
A repeatable shape or an object that is used to fill objects or applied to brush strokes to a path.

Pencil tool
A drawing tool that enables you to draw paths and adjust the paths by editing their anchor points.

perspective drawing
A drawing that depicts depth in a two-dimensional image.

perspective grid
A set of lines that helps you create drawings with depth.

Photoshop effect
An effect that you can apply to both vector and bitmap objects.

pixel grid
A set of vertical and horizontal lines that is used to align objects when you set pixels as the unit of measurement for your document. By using the pixel grid, you can ensure that objects begin and end on a whole pixel.

Pixel Preview
A mode that displays the pixel grid and appearance of rasterized graphics on the grid.

print preset
A predetermined collection of settings for the options in the Print dialog box.

process color
A color that uses a combination of cyan, magenta, yellow, and black ink to produce all other colors.

Shape Builder tool
A tool that allows creation of custom shapes by merging shapes or by deleting areas of a shape.

slice
A portion of a large image that can be saved as an independent file with its own format and settings.

smart guide
A guide that is displayed when you draw, align, or transform objects.

spot color
A color that uses a single ink to display color accurately and consistently.

SVG
(Scalable Vector Graphics) An XML-based image file format used to save two-dimensional static or dynamic vector graphics.

swatch
A named color, gradient, or pattern that can be selected from the Swatches panel to fill and stroke objects.

symbol
An object that serves as a template to quickly create identical objects.

symbol library
A collection of preset symbols that appear in a panel of their own.

symbol registration point
A visible mark that serves as the origin of a symbol.

symbol set
A group of symbol instances that can be added to artwork and modified using symbolism tools.

trapping
A technique that is used to print adjoining colors without any gaps among the colors.

Index